TRADING JOURNAL

This book belongs to:

_____

Trading Log X 81 Pages

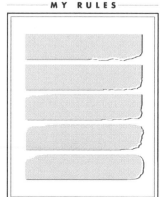

MY RULES

MY OWN TABLE OF CONTENTS

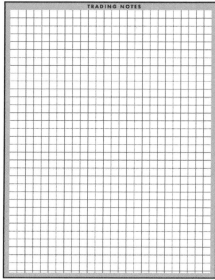

TRADING NOTES X 13 Pages
(Graph Note Quad Ruled 4x4 in 1Inch)

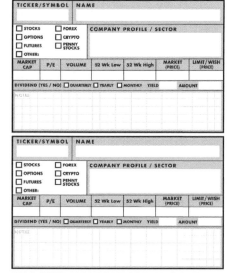

STOCKS WATCHLIST X 20 Pages (40 Tickers)

MONTHLY TRADING RESULTS

TABLE OF CONTENTS

TICKER/SYMBOL

NAME

- ☐ STOCKS
- ☐ OPTIONS
- ☐ FUTURES
- ☐ OTHER:
- ☐ FOREX
- ☐ CRYPTO
- ☐ PENNY STOCKS

COMPANY PROFILE / NOTES

MARKET PLATFORMS	FEES

DIVIDEND (YES / NO)   ☐ QUARTERLY   ☐ YEARLY   ☐ MONTHLY

YIELD										
AMOUNT										
PAY DATE										

DATE	TYPE		PRICE	QUANTITY #	COST	NET GAIN (LOSS)	AVERAGE COST	%
	BUY	SELL						
TOTAL GAIN (LOSS)					TOTAL% GAIN (LOSS)			%

TRADING NOTES

TICKER/SYMBOL	NAME

- ☐ STOCKS ☐ FOREX
- ☐ OPTIONS ☐ CRYPTO
- ☐ FUTURES ☐ PENNY STOCKS
- ☐ OTHER:

COMPANY PROFILE / NOTES

MARKET PLATFORMS	FEES

DIVIDEND (YES / NO)   ☐ QUARTERLY   ☐ YEARLY   ☐ MONTHLY

YIELD											
AMOUNT											
PAY DATE											

DATE	TYPE		PRICE	QUANTITY #	COST	NET GAIN (LOSS)	AVERAGE COST	%
	BUY	SELL						
TOTAL GAIN (LOSS)					TOTAL% GAIN (LOSS)			%

TRADING NOTES

TICKER/SYMBOL

NAME

- ☐ STOCKS
- ☐ OPTIONS
- ☐ FUTURES
- ☐ OTHER:
- ☐ FOREX
- ☐ CRYPTO
- ☐ PENNY STOCKS

COMPANY PROFILE / NOTES

MARKET PLATFORMS	FEES

DIVIDEND (YES / NO)   ☐ QUARTERLY   ☐ YEARLY   ☐ MONTHLY

YIELD										
AMOUNT										
PAY DATE										

DATE	TYPE		PRICE	QUANTITY #	COST	NET GAIN (LOSS)	AVERAGE COST	%
	BUY	SELL						
TOTAL GAIN (LOSS)					TOTAL% GAIN (LOSS)			%

TRADING NOTES

TICKER/SYMBOL

NAME

- [ ] STOCKS
- [ ] OPTIONS
- [ ] FUTURES
- [ ] OTHER:
- [ ] FOREX
- [ ] CRYPTO
- [ ] PENNY STOCKS

COMPANY PROFILE / NOTES

MARKET PLATFORMS	FEES

DIVIDEND (YES / NO)   [ ] QUARTERLY   [ ] YEARLY   [ ] MONTHLY

YIELD									
AMOUNT									
PAY DATE									

DATE	TYPE		PRICE	QUANTITY #	COST	NET GAIN (LOSS)	AVERAGE COST	%
	BUY	SELL						
TOTAL GAIN (LOSS)					TOTAL% GAIN (LOSS)			%

TRADING NOTES

TICKER/SYMBOL

NAME

- ☐ STOCKS
- ☐ OPTIONS
- ☐ FUTURES
- ☐ OTHER:
- ☐ FOREX
- ☐ CRYPTO
- ☐ PENNY STOCKS

COMPANY PROFILE / NOTES

MARKET PLATFORMS	FEES

DIVIDEND (YES / NO)   ☐ QUARTERLY   ☐ YEARLY   ☐ MONTHLY

YIELD											
AMOUNT											
PAY DATE											

DATE	TYPE		PRICE	QUANTITY #	COST	NET GAIN (LOSS)	AVERAGE COST	%
	BUY	SELL						
TOTAL GAIN (LOSS)					TOTAL% GAIN (LOSS)			%

TRADING NOTES

TICKER/SYMBOL

NAME

- [ ] STOCKS
- [ ] OPTIONS
- [ ] FUTURES
- [ ] OTHER:
- [ ] FOREX
- [ ] CRYPTO
- [ ] PENNY STOCKS

COMPANY PROFILE / NOTES

MARKET PLATFORMS	FEES

DIVIDEND (YES / NO)   [ ] QUARTERLY   [ ] YEARLY   [ ] MONTHLY

YIELD											
AMOUNT											
PAY DATE											

DATE	TYPE		PRICE	QUANTITY #	COST	NET GAIN (LOSS)	AVERAGE COST	%
	BUY	SELL						
TOTAL GAIN (LOSS)					TOTAL% GAIN (LOSS)			%

TRADING NOTES

TICKER/SYMBOL

NAME

- ☐ STOCKS
- ☐ OPTIONS
- ☐ FUTURES
- ☐ OTHER:
- ☐ FOREX
- ☐ CRYPTO
- ☐ PENNY STOCKS

COMPANY PROFILE / NOTES

MARKET PLATFORMS	FEES

DIVIDEND (YES / NO) ☐ QUARTERLY ☐ YEARLY ☐ MONTHLY

YIELD											
AMOUNT											
PAY DATE											

DATE	TYPE		PRICE	QUANTITY #	COST	NET GAIN (LOSS)	AVERAGE COST	%
	BUY	SELL						
TOTAL GAIN (LOSS)					TOTAL% GAIN (LOSS)			%

TRADING NOTES

TICKER/SYMBOL	NAME

STOCKS	☐	FOREX ☐
OPTIONS ☐	CRYPTO ☐
FUTURES ☐	PENNY STOCKS ☐
OTHER: ☐	

COMPANY PROFILE / NOTES

MARKET PLATFORMS	FEES

DIVIDEND (YES / NO) ☐ QUARTERLY ☐ YEARLY ☐ MONTHLY

YIELD										
AMOUNT										
PAY DATE										

DATE	TYPE		PRICE	QUANTITY #	COST	NET GAIN (LOSS)	AVERAGE COST	%
	BUY	SELL						
TOTAL GAIN (LOSS)				TOTAL% GAIN (LOSS)				%

TRADING NOTES

12

TICKER/SYMBOL

NAME

- [ ] STOCKS
- [ ] OPTIONS
- [ ] FUTURES
- [ ] OTHER:
- [ ] FOREX
- [ ] CRYPTO
- [ ] PENNY STOCKS

COMPANY PROFILE / NOTES

MARKET PLATFORMS	FEES

DIVIDEND (YES / NO)   [ ] QUARTERLY   [ ] YEARLY   [ ] MONTHLY

YIELD											
AMOUNT											
PAY DATE											

DATE	TYPE		PRICE	QUANTITY #	COST	NET GAIN (LOSS)	AVERAGE COST	%
	BUY	SELL						
TOTAL GAIN (LOSS)					TOTAL% GAIN (LOSS)			%

TRADING NOTES

TICKER/SYMBOL	NAME

STOCKS	FOREX
☐ STOCKS	☐ FOREX
☐ OPTIONS	☐ CRYPTO
☐ FUTURES	☐ PENNY STOCKS
☐ OTHER:	

COMPANY PROFILE / NOTES

MARKET PLATFORMS	FEES

DIVIDEND (YES / NO) ☐ QUARTERLY ☐ YEARLY ☐ MONTHLY

YIELD									
AMOUNT									
PAY DATE									

DATE	TYPE		PRICE	QUANTITY #	COST	NET GAIN (LOSS)	AVERAGE COST	%
	BUY	SELL						
TOTAL GAIN (LOSS)					TOTAL% GAIN (LOSS)			%

TRADING NOTES

TICKER/SYMBOL	NAME

☐ STOCKS   ☐ FOREX

☐ OPTIONS   ☐ CRYPTO

☐ FUTURES   ☐ PENNY STOCKS

☐ OTHER:

COMPANY PROFILE / NOTES

MARKET PLATFORMS	FEES

DIVIDEND (YES / NO)   ☐ QUARTERLY   ☐ YEARLY   ☐ MONTHLY

YIELD											
AMOUNT											
PAY DATE											

DATE	TYPE		PRICE	QUANTITY #	COST	NET GAIN (LOSS)	AVERAGE COST	%
	BUY	SELL						
TOTAL GAIN (LOSS)					TOTAL% GAIN (LOSS)			%

TRADING NOTES

TICKER/SYMBOL	NAME

- [ ] STOCKS
- [ ] OPTIONS
- [ ] FUTURES
- [ ] OTHER:
- [ ] FOREX
- [ ] CRYPTO
- [ ] PENNY STOCKS

COMPANY PROFILE / NOTES

MARKET PLATFORMS	FEES

DIVIDEND (YES / NO)   ☐ QUARTERLY   ☐ YEARLY   ☐ MONTHLY

YIELD												
AMOUNT												
PAY DATE												

DATE	TYPE		PRICE	QUANTITY #	COST	NET GAIN (LOSS)	AVERAGE COST	%
	BUY	SELL						
TOTAL GAIN (LOSS)					TOTAL% GAIN (LOSS)			%

TRADING NOTES

TICKER/SYMBOL

NAME

- [ ] STOCKS
- [ ] OPTIONS
- [ ] FUTURES
- [ ] OTHER:
- [ ] FOREX
- [ ] CRYPTO
- [ ] PENNY STOCKS

COMPANY PROFILE / NOTES

MARKET PLATFORMS	FEES

DIVIDEND (YES / NO)   [ ] QUARTERLY   [ ] YEARLY   [ ] MONTHLY

YIELD											
AMOUNT											
PAY DATE											

DATE	TYPE		PRICE	QUANTITY #	COST	NET GAIN (LOSS)	AVERAGE COST	%
	BUY	SELL						
TOTAL GAIN (LOSS)					**TOTAL% GAIN (LOSS)**			%

TRADING NOTES

TICKER/SYMBOL

NAME

- ☐ STOCKS
- ☐ OPTIONS
- ☐ FUTURES
- ☐ OTHER:
- ☐ FOREX
- ☐ CRYPTO
- ☐ PENNY STOCKS

COMPANY PROFILE / NOTES

MARKET PLATFORMS	FEES

DIVIDEND (YES / NO)   ☐ QUARTERLY   ☐ YEARLY   ☐ MONTHLY

YIELD												
AMOUNT												
PAY DATE												

DATE	TYPE		PRICE	QUANTITY #	COST	NET GAIN (LOSS)	AVERAGE COST	%
	BUY	SELL						
TOTAL GAIN (LOSS)					TOTAL% GAIN (LOSS)			%

TRADING NOTES

TICKER/SYMBOL

NAME

- ☐ STOCKS
- ☐ OPTIONS
- ☐ FUTURES
- ☐ OTHER:
- ☐ FOREX
- ☐ CRYPTO
- ☐ PENNY STOCKS

COMPANY PROFILE / NOTES

MARKET PLATFORMS	FEES

DIVIDEND (YES / NO) ☐ QUARTERLY ☐ YEARLY ☐ MONTHLY

YIELD											
AMOUNT											
PAY DATE											

DATE	TYPE		PRICE	QUANTITY #	COST	NET GAIN (LOSS)	AVERAGE COST	%
	BUY	SELL						
TOTAL GAIN (LOSS)					TOTAL% GAIN (LOSS)			%

TRADING NOTES

TICKER/SYMBOL	NAME

STOCKS ☐   **FOREX** ☐
OPTIONS ☐   **CRYPTO** ☐
FUTURES ☐   **PENNY STOCKS** ☐
OTHER: ☐

COMPANY PROFILE / NOTES

MARKET PLATFORMS	FEES

DIVIDEND (YES / NO)   ☐ QUARTERLY   ☐ YEARLY   ☐ MONTHLY

YIELD											
AMOUNT											
PAY DATE											

DATE	TYPE		PRICE	QUANTITY #	COST	NET GAIN (LOSS)	AVERAGE COST	%
	BUY	SELL						
TOTAL GAIN (LOSS)					**TOTAL% GAIN (LOSS)**			%

TRADING NOTES

TICKER/SYMBOL	NAME

STOCKS ☐ **FOREX** ☐
OPTIONS ☐ **CRYPTO** ☐
FUTURES ☐ **PENNY STOCKS** ☐
OTHER: ☐

COMPANY PROFILE / NOTES

MARKET PLATFORMS	FEES

DIVIDEND (YES / NO) ☐ QUARTERLY ☐ YEARLY ☐ MONTHLY

YIELD										
AMOUNT										
PAY DATE										

DATE	TYPE		PRICE	QUANTITY #	COST	NET GAIN (LOSS)	AVERAGE COST	%
	BUY	SELL						
TOTAL GAIN (LOSS)					TOTAL% GAIN (LOSS)			%

TRADING NOTES

TICKER/SYMBOL

NAME

- ☐ STOCKS
- ☐ OPTIONS
- ☐ FUTURES
- ☐ OTHER:
- ☐ FOREX
- ☐ CRYPTO
- ☐ PENNY STOCKS

COMPANY PROFILE / NOTES

MARKET PLATFORMS	FEES

DIVIDEND (YES / NO)	☐ QUARTERLY	☐ YEARLY	☐ MONTHLY

YIELD										
AMOUNT										
PAY DATE										

DATE	TYPE		PRICE	QUANTITY #	COST	NET GAIN (LOSS)	AVERAGE COST	%
	BUY	SELL						
TOTAL GAIN (LOSS)					TOTAL% GAIN (LOSS)			%

TRADING NOTES

TICKER/SYMBOL

NAME

- ☐ STOCKS
- ☐ OPTIONS
- ☐ FUTURES
- ☐ OTHER:
- ☐ FOREX
- ☐ CRYPTO
- ☐ PENNY STOCKS

COMPANY PROFILE / NOTES

MARKET PLATFORMS	FEES

DIVIDEND (YES / NO)   ☐ QUARTERLY   ☐ YEARLY   ☐ MONTHLY

YIELD										
AMOUNT										
PAY DATE										

DATE	TYPE		PRICE	QUANTITY #	COST	NET GAIN (LOSS)	AVERAGE COST	%
	BUY	SELL						
TOTAL GAIN (LOSS)					TOTAL% GAIN (LOSS)			%

TRADING NOTES

TICKER/SYMBOL	NAME

- [ ] STOCKS
- [ ] OPTIONS
- [ ] FUTURES
- [ ] OTHER:
- [ ] FOREX
- [ ] CRYPTO
- [ ] PENNY STOCKS

COMPANY PROFILE / NOTES

MARKET PLATFORMS	FEES

DIVIDEND (YES / NO)   [ ] QUARTERLY   [ ] YEARLY   [ ] MONTHLY

YIELD										
AMOUNT										
PAY DATE										

DATE	TYPE		PRICE	QUANTITY #	COST	NET GAIN (LOSS)	AVERAGE COST	%
	BUY	SELL						
TOTAL GAIN (LOSS)					TOTAL% GAIN (LOSS)			%

TRADING NOTES

TICKER/SYMBOL

NAME

- [ ] STOCKS
- [ ] OPTIONS
- [ ] FUTURES
- [ ] OTHER:
- [ ] FOREX
- [ ] CRYPTO
- [ ] PENNY STOCKS

COMPANY PROFILE / NOTES

MARKET PLATFORMS	FEES

DIVIDEND (YES / NO)　　[ ] QUARTERLY　　[ ] YEARLY　　[ ] MONTHLY

YIELD										
AMOUNT										
PAY DATE										

DATE	TYPE		PRICE	QUANTITY #	COST	NET GAIN (LOSS)	AVERAGE COST	%
	BUY	SELL						
TOTAL GAIN (LOSS)					TOTAL% GAIN (LOSS)			%

TRADING NOTES

TICKER/SYMBOL	NAME

- ☐ STOCKS   ☐ FOREX
- ☐ OPTIONS   ☐ CRYPTO
- ☐ FUTURES   ☐ PENNY STOCKS
- ☐ OTHER:

COMPANY PROFILE / NOTES

MARKET PLATFORMS	FEES

DIVIDEND (YES / NO)   ☐ QUARTERLY   ☐ YEARLY   ☐ MONTHLY

YIELD										
AMOUNT										
PAY DATE										

DATE	TYPE BUY	TYPE SELL	PRICE	QUANTITY #	COST	NET GAIN (LOSS)	AVERAGE COST	%
TOTAL GAIN (LOSS)					TOTAL% GAIN (LOSS)			%

TRADING NOTES

TICKER/SYMBOL

NAME

- [ ] STOCKS
- [ ] OPTIONS
- [ ] FUTURES
- [ ] OTHER:
- [ ] FOREX
- [ ] CRYPTO
- [ ] PENNY STOCKS

COMPANY PROFILE / NOTES

MARKET PLATFORMS	FEES

DIVIDEND (YES / NO)   [ ] QUARTERLY   [ ] YEARLY   [ ] MONTHLY

YIELD									
AMOUNT									
PAY DATE									

DATE	TYPE		PRICE	QUANTITY #	COST	NET GAIN (LOSS)	AVERAGE COST	%
	BUY	SELL						
TOTAL GAIN (LOSS)					TOTAL% GAIN (LOSS)			%

TRADING NOTES

TICKER/SYMBOL

NAME

- ☐ STOCKS
- ☐ OPTIONS
- ☐ FUTURES
- ☐ OTHER:
- ☐ FOREX
- ☐ CRYPTO
- ☐ PENNY STOCKS

COMPANY PROFILE / NOTES

MARKET PLATFORMS	FEES

DIVIDEND (YES / NO)   ☐ QUARTERLY   ☐ YEARLY   ☐ MONTHLY

YIELD											
AMOUNT											
PAY DATE											

DATE	TYPE		PRICE	QUANTITY #	COST	NET GAIN (LOSS)	AVERAGE COST	%
	BUY	SELL						
TOTAL GAIN (LOSS)					TOTAL% GAIN (LOSS)			%

TRADING NOTES

TICKER/SYMBOL

NAME

- ☐ STOCKS
- ☐ OPTIONS
- ☐ FUTURES
- ☐ OTHER:
- ☐ FOREX
- ☐ CRYPTO
- ☐ PENNY STOCKS

COMPANY PROFILE / NOTES

MARKET PLATFORMS	FEES

DIVIDEND (YES / NO)   ☐ QUARTERLY   ☐ YEARLY   ☐ MONTHLY

YIELD											
AMOUNT											
PAY DATE											

DATE	TYPE		PRICE	QUANTITY #	COST	NET GAIN (LOSS)	AVERAGE COST	%
	BUY	SELL						
TOTAL GAIN (LOSS)				TOTAL% GAIN (LOSS)				%

TRADING NOTES

TICKER/SYMBOL

NAME

- ☐ STOCKS
- ☐ OPTIONS
- ☐ FUTURES
- ☐ OTHER:
- ☐ FOREX
- ☐ CRYPTO
- ☐ PENNY STOCKS

COMPANY PROFILE / NOTES

MARKET PLATFORMS	FEES

DIVIDEND (YES / NO)   ☐ QUARTERLY   ☐ YEARLY   ☐ MONTHLY

YIELD											
AMOUNT											
PAY DATE											

DATE	TYPE		PRICE	QUANTITY #	COST	NET GAIN (LOSS)	AVERAGE COST	%
	BUY	SELL						
TOTAL GAIN (LOSS)					TOTAL% GAIN (LOSS)			%

TRADING NOTES

TICKER/SYMBOL

NAME

- [ ] STOCKS
- [ ] OPTIONS
- [ ] FUTURES
- [ ] OTHER:
- [ ] FOREX
- [ ] CRYPTO
- [ ] PENNY STOCKS

COMPANY PROFILE / NOTES

MARKET PLATFORMS	FEES

DIVIDEND (YES / NO)   [ ] QUARTERLY   [ ] YEARLY   [ ] MONTHLY

YIELD											
AMOUNT											
PAY DATE											

DATE	TYPE		PRICE	QUANTITY #	COST	NET GAIN (LOSS)	AVERAGE COST	%
	BUY	SELL						
TOTAL GAIN (LOSS)					TOTAL% GAIN (LOSS)			%

TRADING NOTES

TICKER/SYMBOL

NAME

- ☐ STOCKS
- ☐ OPTIONS
- ☐ FUTURES
- ☐ OTHER:
- ☐ FOREX
- ☐ CRYPTO
- ☐ PENNY STOCKS

COMPANY PROFILE / NOTES

MARKET PLATFORMS	FEES

DIVIDEND (YES / NO)   ☐ QUARTERLY   ☐ YEARLY   ☐ MONTHLY

YIELD											
AMOUNT											
PAY DATE											

DATE	TYPE		PRICE	QUANTITY #	COST	NET GAIN (LOSS)	AVERAGE COST	%
	BUY	SELL						
TOTAL GAIN (LOSS)					TOTAL% GAIN (LOSS)			%

TRADING NOTES

32

TICKER/SYMBOL	NAME

☐ STOCKS ☐ FOREX	**COMPANY PROFILE / NOTES**
☐ OPTIONS ☐ CRYPTO	
☐ FUTURES ☐ PENNY STOCKS	
☐ OTHER:	

MARKET PLATFORMS	FEES

DIVIDEND (YES / NO)   ☐ QUARTERLY   ☐ YEARLY   ☐ MONTHLY

YIELD											
AMOUNT											
PAY DATE											

DATE	TYPE		PRICE	QUANTITY #	COST	NET GAIN (LOSS)	AVERAGE COST	%
	BUY	SELL						
TOTAL GAIN (LOSS)					**TOTAL% GAIN (LOSS)**			%

TRADING NOTES

TICKER/SYMBOL

NAME

- [ ] STOCKS
- [ ] OPTIONS
- [ ] FUTURES
- [ ] OTHER:
- [ ] FOREX
- [ ] CRYPTO
- [ ] PENNY STOCKS

COMPANY PROFILE / NOTES

MARKET PLATFORMS	FEES

DIVIDEND (YES / NO)   [ ] QUARTERLY   [ ] YEARLY   [ ] MONTHLY

YIELD									
AMOUNT									
PAY DATE									

DATE	TYPE		PRICE	QUANTITY #	COST	NET GAIN (LOSS)	AVERAGE COST	%
	BUY	SELL						
TOTAL GAIN (LOSS)					TOTAL% GAIN (LOSS)			%

TRADING NOTES

TICKER/SYMBOL

NAME

- ☐ STOCKS
- ☐ OPTIONS
- ☐ FUTURES
- ☐ OTHER:
- ☐ FOREX
- ☐ CRYPTO
- ☐ PENNY STOCKS

COMPANY PROFILE / NOTES

MARKET PLATFORMS	FEES

DIVIDEND (YES / NO)   ☐ QUARTERLY   ☐ YEARLY   ☐ MONTHLY

YIELD											
AMOUNT											
PAY DATE											

DATE	TYPE		PRICE	QUANTITY #	COST	NET GAIN (LOSS)	AVERAGE COST	%
	BUY	SELL						
TOTAL GAIN (LOSS)					TOTAL% GAIN (LOSS)			%

TRADING NOTES

TICKER/SYMBOL	NAME

- ☐ STOCKS
- ☐ OPTIONS
- ☐ FUTURES
- ☐ OTHER:
- ☐ FOREX
- ☐ CRYPTO
- ☐ PENNY STOCKS

COMPANY PROFILE / NOTES

MARKET PLATFORMS	FEES

DIVIDEND (YES / NO)   ☐ QUARTERLY   ☐ YEARLY   ☐ MONTHLY

YIELD											
AMOUNT											
PAY DATE											

DATE	TYPE		PRICE	QUANTITY #	COST	NET GAIN (LOSS)	AVERAGE COST	%
	BUY	SELL						
TOTAL GAIN (LOSS)					TOTAL% GAIN (LOSS)			%

TRADING NOTES

TICKER/SYMBOL

NAME

- [ ] STOCKS
- [ ] OPTIONS
- [ ] FUTURES
- [ ] OTHER:
- [ ] FOREX
- [ ] CRYPTO
- [ ] PENNY STOCKS

COMPANY PROFILE / NOTES

MARKET PLATFORMS	FEES

DIVIDEND (YES / NO) □ QUARTERLY □ YEARLY □ MONTHLY

YIELD										
AMOUNT										
PAY DATE										

DATE	TYPE		PRICE	QUANTITY #	COST	NET GAIN (LOSS)	AVERAGE COST	%
	BUY	SELL						
TOTAL GAIN (LOSS)					TOTAL% GAIN (LOSS)			%

TRADING NOTES

TICKER/SYMBOL

NAME

- ☐ STOCKS
- ☐ OPTIONS
- ☐ FUTURES
- ☐ OTHER:
- ☐ FOREX
- ☐ CRYPTO
- ☐ PENNY STOCKS

COMPANY PROFILE / NOTES

MARKET PLATFORMS	FEES

DIVIDEND (YES / NO)   ☐ QUARTERLY   ☐ YEARLY   ☐ MONTHLY

YIELD											
AMOUNT											
PAY DATE											

DATE	TYPE		PRICE	QUANTITY #	COST	NET GAIN (LOSS)	AVERAGE COST	%
	BUY	SELL						
TOTAL GAIN (LOSS)					TOTAL% GAIN (LOSS)			%

TRADING NOTES

TICKER/SYMBOL

NAME

- ☐ STOCKS
- ☐ OPTIONS
- ☐ FUTURES
- ☐ OTHER:
- ☐ FOREX
- ☐ CRYPTO
- ☐ PENNY STOCKS

COMPANY PROFILE / NOTES

MARKET PLATFORMS	FEES

DIVIDEND (YES / NO)   ☐ QUARTERLY   ☐ YEARLY   ☐ MONTHLY

YIELD											
AMOUNT											
PAY DATE											

DATE	TYPE		PRICE	QUANTITY #	COST	NET GAIN (LOSS)	AVERAGE COST	%
	BUY	SELL						
TOTAL GAIN (LOSS)				TOTAL% GAIN (LOSS)				%

TRADING NOTES

TICKER/SYMBOL	NAME

☐ STOCKS ☐ FOREX	**COMPANY PROFILE / NOTES**
☐ OPTIONS ☐ CRYPTO	
☐ FUTURES ☐ PENNY STOCKS	
☐ OTHER:	

MARKET PLATFORMS	FEES

DIVIDEND (YES / NO)	☐ QUARTERLY	☐ YEARLY	☐ MONTHLY

YIELD											
AMOUNT											
PAY DATE											

DATE	TYPE		PRICE	QUANTITY #	COST	NET GAIN (LOSS)	AVERAGE COST	%
	BUY	SELL						
TOTAL GAIN (LOSS)					**TOTAL% GAIN (LOSS)**			%

TRADING NOTES

TICKER/SYMBOL	NAME

STOCKS ☐ **FOREX** ☐
OPTIONS ☐ **CRYPTO** ☐
FUTURES ☐ **PENNY STOCKS** ☐
OTHER: ☐

COMPANY PROFILE / NOTES

MARKET PLATFORMS	FEES

DIVIDEND (YES / NO)   ☐ QUARTERLY   ☐ YEARLY   ☐ MONTHLY

YIELD									
AMOUNT									
PAY DATE									

DATE	TYPE		PRICE	QUANTITY #	COST	NET GAIN (LOSS)	AVERAGE COST	%
	BUY	SELL						
TOTAL GAIN (LOSS)					TOTAL% GAIN (LOSS)			%

TRADING NOTES

41

TICKER/SYMBOL

NAME

- ☐ STOCKS
- ☐ OPTIONS
- ☐ FUTURES
- ☐ OTHER:
- ☐ FOREX
- ☐ CRYPTO
- ☐ PENNY STOCKS

COMPANY PROFILE / NOTES

MARKET PLATFORMS	FEES

DIVIDEND (YES / NO)   ☐ QUARTERLY   ☐ YEARLY   ☐ MONTHLY

YIELD													
AMOUNT													
PAY DATE													

DATE	TYPE		PRICE	QUANTITY #	COST	NET GAIN (LOSS)	AVERAGE COST	%
	BUY	SELL						
TOTAL GAIN (LOSS)					TOTAL% GAIN (LOSS)			%

TRADING NOTES

TICKER/SYMBOL	NAME

☐ STOCKS ☐ FOREX
☐ OPTIONS ☐ CRYPTO
☐ FUTURES ☐ PENNY STOCKS
☐ OTHER:

COMPANY PROFILE / NOTES

MARKET PLATFORMS	FEES

DIVIDEND (YES / NO) ☐ QUARTERLY ☐ YEARLY ☐ MONTHLY

YIELD										
AMOUNT										
PAY DATE										

DATE	TYPE		PRICE	QUANTITY #	COST	NET GAIN (LOSS)	AVERAGE COST	%
	BUY	SELL						
TOTAL GAIN (LOSS)				TOTAL% GAIN (LOSS)				%

TRADING NOTES

TICKER/SYMBOL	NAME

STOCKS ☐   **FOREX** ☐

OPTIONS ☐   **CRYPTO** ☐

FUTURES ☐   **PENNY STOCKS** ☐

OTHER: ☐

COMPANY PROFILE / NOTES

MARKET PLATFORMS	FEES

DIVIDEND (YES / NO) ☐ QUARTERLY ☐ YEARLY ☐ MONTHLY

YIELD									
AMOUNT									
PAY DATE									

DATE	TYPE		PRICE	QUANTITY #	COST	NET GAIN (LOSS)	AVERAGE COST	%
	BUY	SELL						
TOTAL GAIN (LOSS)					**TOTAL% GAIN (LOSS)**			%

TRADING NOTES

TICKER/SYMBOL

NAME

- ☐ STOCKS
- ☐ OPTIONS
- ☐ FUTURES
- ☐ OTHER:
- ☐ FOREX
- ☐ CRYPTO
- ☐ PENNY STOCKS

COMPANY PROFILE / NOTES

MARKET PLATFORMS	FEES

DIVIDEND (YES / NO) ☐ QUARTERLY ☐ YEARLY ☐ MONTHLY

YIELD											
AMOUNT											
PAY DATE											

DATE	TYPE		PRICE	QUANTITY #	COST	NET GAIN (LOSS)	AVERAGE COST	%
	BUY	SELL						
TOTAL GAIN (LOSS)					TOTAL% GAIN (LOSS)			%

TRADING NOTES

TICKER/SYMBOL

NAME

- ☐ STOCKS
- ☐ OPTIONS
- ☐ FUTURES
- ☐ OTHER:
- ☐ FOREX
- ☐ CRYPTO
- ☐ PENNY STOCKS

COMPANY PROFILE / NOTES

MARKET PLATFORMS	FEES

DIVIDEND (YES / NO)   ☐ QUARTERLY   ☐ YEARLY   ☐ MONTHLY

YIELD									
AMOUNT									
PAY DATE									

DATE	TYPE		PRICE	QUANTITY #	COST	NET GAIN (LOSS)	AVERAGE COST	%
	BUY	SELL						
TOTAL GAIN (LOSS)					TOTAL% GAIN (LOSS)			%

TRADING NOTES

TICKER/SYMBOL

NAME

- ☐ STOCKS
- ☐ OPTIONS
- ☐ FUTURES
- ☐ OTHER:
- ☐ FOREX
- ☐ CRYPTO
- ☐ PENNY STOCKS

COMPANY PROFILE / NOTES

MARKET PLATFORMS	FEES

DIVIDEND (YES / NO)　☐ QUARTERLY　☐ YEARLY　☐ MONTHLY

YIELD									
AMOUNT									
PAY DATE									

DATE	TYPE BUY	TYPE SELL	PRICE	QUANTITY #	COST	NET GAIN (LOSS)	AVERAGE COST	%
TOTAL GAIN (LOSS)					TOTAL% GAIN (LOSS)			%

TRADING NOTES

TICKER/SYMBOL	NAME

- ☐ STOCKS
- ☐ OPTIONS
- ☐ FUTURES
- ☐ OTHER:
- ☐ FOREX
- ☐ CRYPTO
- ☐ PENNY STOCKS

COMPANY PROFILE / NOTES

MARKET PLATFORMS	FEES

DIVIDEND (YES / NO)	☐ QUARTERLY	☐ YEARLY	☐ MONTHLY

YIELD											
AMOUNT											
PAY DATE											

DATE	TYPE		PRICE	QUANTITY #	COST	NET GAIN (LOSS)	AVERAGE COST	%
	BUY	SELL						
TOTAL GAIN (LOSS)					TOTAL% GAIN (LOSS)			%

TRADING NOTES

TICKER/SYMBOL	NAME

STOCKS ☐ **FOREX** ☐
OPTIONS ☐ **CRYPTO** ☐
FUTURES ☐ **PENNY STOCKS** ☐
OTHER: ☐

COMPANY PROFILE / NOTES

MARKET PLATFORMS	FEES

DIVIDEND (YES / NO)   ☐ QUARTERLY   ☐ YEARLY   ☐ MONTHLY

YIELD									
AMOUNT									
PAY DATE									

DATE	TYPE		PRICE	QUANTITY #	COST	NET GAIN (LOSS)	AVERAGE COST	%
	BUY	SELL						
TOTAL GAIN (LOSS)					TOTAL% GAIN (LOSS)			%

TRADING NOTES

TICKER/SYMBOL

NAME

- [ ] STOCKS
- [ ] OPTIONS
- [ ] FUTURES
- [ ] OTHER:
- [ ] FOREX
- [ ] CRYPTO
- [ ] PENNY STOCKS

COMPANY PROFILE / NOTES

MARKET PLATFORMS	FEES

DIVIDEND (YES / NO)   □ QUARTERLY   □ YEARLY   □ MONTHLY

YIELD											
AMOUNT											
PAY DATE											

DATE	TYPE		PRICE	QUANTITY #	COST	NET GAIN (LOSS)	AVERAGE COST	%
	BUY	SELL						
TOTAL GAIN (LOSS)					TOTAL% GAIN (LOSS)			%

TRADING NOTES

TICKER/SYMBOL

NAME

- [ ] STOCKS
- [ ] OPTIONS
- [ ] FUTURES
- [ ] OTHER:
- [ ] FOREX
- [ ] CRYPTO
- [ ] PENNY STOCKS

COMPANY PROFILE / NOTES

MARKET PLATFORMS	FEES

DIVIDEND (YES / NO)   [ ] QUARTERLY   [ ] YEARLY   [ ] MONTHLY

YIELD										
AMOUNT										
PAY DATE										

DATE	TYPE		PRICE	QUANTITY #	COST	NET GAIN (LOSS)	AVERAGE COST	%
	BUY	SELL						
TOTAL GAIN (LOSS)					TOTAL% GAIN (LOSS)			%

TRADING NOTES

TICKER/SYMBOL	NAME

STOCKS ☐ **FOREX** ☐
OPTIONS ☐ **CRYPTO** ☐
FUTURES ☐ **PENNY STOCKS** ☐
OTHER: ☐

COMPANY PROFILE / NOTES

MARKET PLATFORMS	FEES

DIVIDEND (YES / NO) ☐ QUARTERLY ☐ YEARLY ☐ MONTHLY

YIELD										
AMOUNT										
PAY DATE										

DATE	TYPE		PRICE	QUANTITY #	COST	NET GAIN (LOSS)	AVERAGE COST	%
	BUY	SELL						
TOTAL GAIN (LOSS)					**TOTAL% GAIN (LOSS)**			%

TRADING NOTES

TICKER/SYMBOL

NAME

- ☐ STOCKS
- ☐ OPTIONS
- ☐ FUTURES
- ☐ OTHER:
- ☐ FOREX
- ☐ CRYPTO
- ☐ PENNY STOCKS

COMPANY PROFILE / NOTES

MARKET PLATFORMS	FEES

DIVIDEND (YES / NO)   ☐ QUARTERLY   ☐ YEARLY   ☐ MONTHLY

YIELD										
AMOUNT										
PAY DATE										

DATE	TYPE		PRICE	QUANTITY #	COST	NET GAIN (LOSS)	AVERAGE COST	%
	BUY	SELL						
TOTAL GAIN (LOSS)					TOTAL% GAIN (LOSS)			%

TRADING NOTES

53

TICKER/SYMBOL	NAME

- ☐ STOCKS ☐ FOREX
- ☐ OPTIONS ☐ CRYPTO
- ☐ FUTURES ☐ PENNY STOCKS
- ☐ OTHER:

COMPANY PROFILE / NOTES

MARKET PLATFORMS	FEES

DIVIDEND (YES / NO)   ☐ QUARTERLY   ☐ YEARLY   ☐ MONTHLY

YIELD										
AMOUNT										
PAY DATE										

DATE	TYPE		PRICE	QUANTITY #	COST	NET GAIN (LOSS)	AVERAGE COST	%
	BUY	SELL						
TOTAL GAIN (LOSS)					TOTAL% GAIN (LOSS)			%

TRADING NOTES

TICKER/SYMBOL

NAME

- ☐ STOCKS
- ☐ OPTIONS
- ☐ FUTURES
- ☐ OTHER:
- ☐ FOREX
- ☐ CRYPTO
- ☐ PENNY STOCKS

COMPANY PROFILE / NOTES

MARKET PLATFORMS	FEES

DIVIDEND (YES / NO)   ☐ QUARTERLY   ☐ YEARLY   ☐ MONTHLY

YIELD										
AMOUNT										
PAY DATE										

DATE	TYPE		PRICE	QUANTITY #	COST	NET GAIN (LOSS)	AVERAGE COST	%
	BUY	SELL						
TOTAL GAIN (LOSS)				TOTAL% GAIN (LOSS)				%

TRADING NOTES

55

TICKER/SYMBOL

NAME

- [ ] STOCKS
- [ ] OPTIONS
- [ ] FUTURES
- [ ] OTHER:
- [ ] FOREX
- [ ] CRYPTO
- [ ] PENNY STOCKS

COMPANY PROFILE / NOTES

MARKET PLATFORMS	FEES

DIVIDEND (YES / NO)   [ ] QUARTERLY   [ ] YEARLY   [ ] MONTHLY

YIELD											
AMOUNT											
PAY DATE											

DATE	TYPE		PRICE	QUANTITY #	COST	NET GAIN (LOSS)	AVERAGE COST	%
	BUY	SELL						
TOTAL GAIN (LOSS)					TOTAL% GAIN (LOSS)			%

TRADING NOTES

TICKER/SYMBOL

NAME

- ☐ STOCKS
- ☐ OPTIONS
- ☐ FUTURES
- ☐ OTHER:
- ☐ FOREX
- ☐ CRYPTO
- ☐ PENNY STOCKS

COMPANY PROFILE / NOTES

MARKET PLATFORMS	FEES

DIVIDEND (YES / NO)   ☐ QUARTERLY   ☐ YEARLY   ☐ MONTHLY

YIELD										
AMOUNT										
PAY DATE										

DATE	TYPE		PRICE	QUANTITY #	COST	NET GAIN (LOSS)	AVERAGE COST	%
	BUY	SELL						
TOTAL GAIN (LOSS)				TOTAL% GAIN (LOSS)				%

TRADING NOTES

TICKER/SYMBOL

NAME

- [ ] STOCKS
- [ ] OPTIONS
- [ ] FUTURES
- [ ] OTHER:
- [ ] FOREX
- [ ] CRYPTO
- [ ] PENNY STOCKS

COMPANY PROFILE / NOTES

MARKET PLATFORMS	FEES

DIVIDEND (YES / NO)   ☐ QUARTERLY   ☐ YEARLY   ☐ MONTHLY

YIELD										
AMOUNT										
PAY DATE										

DATE	TYPE		PRICE	QUANTITY #	COST	NET GAIN (LOSS)	AVERAGE COST	%
	BUY	SELL						
TOTAL GAIN (LOSS)					TOTAL% GAIN (LOSS)			%

TRADING NOTES

TICKER/SYMBOL

NAME

- ☐ STOCKS
- ☐ OPTIONS
- ☐ FUTURES
- ☐ OTHER:
- ☐ FOREX
- ☐ CRYPTO
- ☐ PENNY STOCKS

COMPANY PROFILE / NOTES

MARKET PLATFORMS	FEES

DIVIDEND (YES / NO)   ☐ QUARTERLY   ☐ YEARLY   ☐ MONTHLY

YIELD										
AMOUNT										
PAY DATE										

DATE	TYPE		PRICE	QUANTITY #	COST	NET GAIN (LOSS)	AVERAGE COST	%
	BUY	SELL						
TOTAL GAIN (LOSS)					TOTAL% GAIN (LOSS)			%

TRADING NOTES

TICKER/SYMBOL

NAME

- ☐ STOCKS
- ☐ OPTIONS
- ☐ FUTURES
- ☐ OTHER:
- ☐ FOREX
- ☐ CRYPTO
- ☐ PENNY STOCKS

COMPANY PROFILE / NOTES

MARKET PLATFORMS	FEES

DIVIDEND (YES / NO)   ☐ QUARTERLY   ☐ YEARLY   ☐ MONTHLY

YIELD										
AMOUNT										
PAY DATE										

DATE	TYPE		PRICE	QUANTITY #	COST	NET GAIN (LOSS)	AVERAGE COST	%
	BUY	SELL						
TOTAL GAIN (LOSS)					TOTAL% GAIN (LOSS)			%

TRADING NOTES

60

TICKER/SYMBOL

NAME

- [ ] STOCKS
- [ ] OPTIONS
- [ ] FUTURES
- [ ] OTHER:
- [ ] FOREX
- [ ] CRYPTO
- [ ] PENNY STOCKS

MARKET PLATFORMS	FEES

COMPANY PROFILE / NOTES

DIVIDEND (YES / NO)   [ ] QUARTERLY   [ ] YEARLY   [ ] MONTHLY

YIELD											
AMOUNT											
PAY DATE											

DATE	TYPE		PRICE	QUANTITY #	COST	NET GAIN (LOSS)	AVERAGE COST	%
	BUY	SELL						
TOTAL GAIN (LOSS)				TOTAL% GAIN (LOSS)				%

TRADING NOTES

61

TICKER/SYMBOL

NAME

- [ ] STOCKS
- [ ] OPTIONS
- [ ] FUTURES
- [ ] OTHER:
- [ ] FOREX
- [ ] CRYPTO
- [ ] PENNY STOCKS

COMPANY PROFILE / NOTES

MARKET PLATFORMS	FEES

DIVIDEND (YES / NO)   [ ] QUARTERLY   [ ] YEARLY   [ ] MONTHLY

YIELD								
AMOUNT								
PAY DATE								

DATE	TYPE		PRICE	QUANTITY #	COST	NET GAIN (LOSS)	AVERAGE COST	%
	BUY	SELL						
TOTAL GAIN (LOSS)					TOTAL% GAIN (LOSS)			%

TRADING NOTES

TICKER/SYMBOL

NAME

- ☐ STOCKS
- ☐ OPTIONS
- ☐ FUTURES
- ☐ OTHER:
- ☐ FOREX
- ☐ CRYPTO
- ☐ PENNY STOCKS

COMPANY PROFILE / NOTES

MARKET PLATFORMS	FEES

DIVIDEND (YES / NO)   ☐ QUARTERLY   ☐ YEARLY   ☐ MONTHLY

YIELD										
AMOUNT										
PAY DATE										

DATE	TYPE		PRICE	QUANTITY #	COST	NET GAIN (LOSS)	AVERAGE COST	%
	BUY	SELL						
TOTAL GAIN (LOSS)					TOTAL% GAIN (LOSS)			%

TRADING NOTES

63

TICKER/SYMBOL

NAME

- ☐ STOCKS
- ☐ OPTIONS
- ☐ FUTURES
- ☐ OTHER:
- ☐ FOREX
- ☐ CRYPTO
- ☐ PENNY STOCKS

COMPANY PROFILE / NOTES

MARKET PLATFORMS	FEES

DIVIDEND (YES / NO)   ☐ QUARTERLY   ☐ YEARLY   ☐ MONTHLY

YIELD											
AMOUNT											
PAY DATE											

DATE	TYPE		PRICE	QUANTITY #	COST	NET GAIN (LOSS)	AVERAGE COST	%
	BUY	SELL						
TOTAL GAIN (LOSS)					TOTAL% GAIN (LOSS)			%

TRADING NOTES

64

TICKER/SYMBOL

NAME

- ☐ STOCKS
- ☐ OPTIONS
- ☐ FUTURES
- ☐ OTHER:
- ☐ FOREX
- ☐ CRYPTO
- ☐ PENNY STOCKS

COMPANY PROFILE / NOTES

MARKET PLATFORMS	FEES

DIVIDEND (YES / NO)	☐ QUARTERLY	☐ YEARLY	☐ MONTHLY

YIELD											
AMOUNT											
PAY DATE											

DATE	TYPE		PRICE	QUANTITY #	COST	NET GAIN (LOSS)	AVERAGE COST	%
	BUY	SELL						
TOTAL GAIN (LOSS)					TOTAL% GAIN (LOSS)			%

TRADING NOTES

TICKER/SYMBOL

NAME

- ☐ STOCKS
- ☐ OPTIONS
- ☐ FUTURES
- ☐ OTHER:
- ☐ FOREX
- ☐ CRYPTO
- ☐ PENNY STOCKS

COMPANY PROFILE / NOTES

MARKET PLATFORMS	FEES

DIVIDEND (YES / NO)   ☐ QUARTERLY   ☐ YEARLY   ☐ MONTHLY

YIELD												
AMOUNT												
PAY DATE												

DATE	TYPE		PRICE	QUANTITY #	COST	NET GAIN (LOSS)	AVERAGE COST	%
	BUY	SELL						
TOTAL GAIN (LOSS)					TOTAL% GAIN (LOSS)			%

TRADING NOTES

TICKER/SYMBOL

NAME

- ☐ STOCKS
- ☐ OPTIONS
- ☐ FUTURES
- ☐ OTHER:
- ☐ FOREX
- ☐ CRYPTO
- ☐ PENNY STOCKS

COMPANY PROFILE / NOTES

MARKET PLATFORMS	FEES

DIVIDEND (YES / NO)   ☐ QUARTERLY   ☐ YEARLY   ☐ MONTHLY

YIELD												
AMOUNT												
PAY DATE												

DATE	TYPE		PRICE	QUANTITY #	COST	NET GAIN (LOSS)	AVERAGE COST	%
	BUY	SELL						
TOTAL GAIN (LOSS)					TOTAL% GAIN (LOSS)			%

TRADING NOTES

TICKER/SYMBOL	NAME

- ☐ STOCKS
- ☐ OPTIONS
- ☐ FUTURES
- ☐ OTHER:
- ☐ FOREX
- ☐ CRYPTO
- ☐ PENNY STOCKS

COMPANY PROFILE / NOTES

MARKET PLATFORMS	FEES

DIVIDEND (YES / NO)   ☐ QUARTERLY   ☐ YEARLY   ☐ MONTHLY

YIELD											
AMOUNT											
PAY DATE											

DATE	TYPE		PRICE	QUANTITY #	COST	NET GAIN (LOSS)	AVERAGE COST	%
	BUY	SELL						
TOTAL GAIN (LOSS)					TOTAL% GAIN (LOSS)			%

TRADING NOTES

TICKER/SYMBOL

NAME

- ☐ STOCKS
- ☐ OPTIONS
- ☐ FUTURES
- ☐ OTHER:
- ☐ FOREX
- ☐ CRYPTO
- ☐ PENNY STOCKS

COMPANY PROFILE / NOTES

MARKET PLATFORMS	FEES

DIVIDEND (YES / NO)   ☐ QUARTERLY   ☐ YEARLY   ☐ MONTHLY

YIELD											
AMOUNT											
PAY DATE											

DATE	TYPE		PRICE	QUANTITY #	COST	NET GAIN (LOSS)	AVERAGE COST	%
	BUY	SELL						
TOTAL GAIN (LOSS)					TOTAL% GAIN (LOSS)			%

TRADING NOTES

TICKER/SYMBOL	NAME

- [ ] STOCKS
- [ ] OPTIONS
- [ ] FUTURES
- [ ] OTHER:
- [ ] FOREX
- [ ] CRYPTO
- [ ] PENNY STOCKS

COMPANY PROFILE / NOTES

MARKET PLATFORMS	FEES

DIVIDEND (YES / NO) [ ] QUARTERLY   [ ] YEARLY   [ ] MONTHLY

YIELD											
AMOUNT											
PAY DATE											

DATE	TYPE BUY	SELL	PRICE	QUANTITY #	COST	NET GAIN (LOSS)	AVERAGE COST	%
TOTAL GAIN (LOSS)					TOTAL% GAIN (LOSS)			%

TRADING NOTES

TICKER/SYMBOL

NAME

- [ ] STOCKS
- [ ] OPTIONS
- [ ] FUTURES
- [ ] OTHER:
- [ ] FOREX
- [ ] CRYPTO
- [ ] PENNY STOCKS

COMPANY PROFILE / NOTES

MARKET PLATFORMS	FEES

DIVIDEND (YES / NO)   [ ] QUARTERLY   [ ] YEARLY   [ ] MONTHLY

YIELD										
AMOUNT										
PAY DATE										

DATE	TYPE		PRICE	QUANTITY #	COST	NET GAIN (LOSS)	AVERAGE COST	%
	BUY	SELL						
TOTAL GAIN (LOSS)					TOTAL% GAIN (LOSS)			%

TRADING NOTES

TICKER/SYMBOL

NAME

- ☐ STOCKS
- ☐ OPTIONS
- ☐ FUTURES
- ☐ OTHER:
- ☐ FOREX
- ☐ CRYPTO
- ☐ PENNY STOCKS

COMPANY PROFILE / NOTES

MARKET PLATFORMS	FEES

DIVIDEND (YES / NO) ☐ QUARTERLY ☐ YEARLY ☐ MONTHLY

YIELD									
AMOUNT									
PAY DATE									

DATE	TYPE		PRICE	QUANTITY #	COST	NET GAIN (LOSS)	AVERAGE COST	%
	BUY	SELL						
TOTAL GAIN (LOSS)					TOTAL% GAIN (LOSS)			%

TRADING NOTES

TICKER/SYMBOL

NAME

- ☐ STOCKS
- ☐ OPTIONS
- ☐ FUTURES
- ☐ OTHER:
- ☐ FOREX
- ☐ CRYPTO
- ☐ PENNY STOCKS

COMPANY PROFILE / NOTES

MARKET PLATFORMS	FEES

DIVIDEND (YES / NO) ☐ QUARTERLY ☐ YEARLY ☐ MONTHLY

YIELD											
AMOUNT											
PAY DATE											

DATE	TYPE		PRICE	QUANTITY #	COST	NET GAIN (LOSS)	AVERAGE COST	%
	BUY	SELL						
TOTAL GAIN (LOSS)					TOTAL% GAIN (LOSS)			%

TRADING NOTES

73

TICKER/SYMBOL

NAME

- ☐ STOCKS
- ☐ OPTIONS
- ☐ FUTURES
- ☐ OTHER:
- ☐ FOREX
- ☐ CRYPTO
- ☐ PENNY STOCKS

COMPANY PROFILE / NOTES

MARKET PLATFORMS	FEES

DIVIDEND (YES / NO)   ☐ QUARTERLY   ☐ YEARLY   ☐ MONTHLY

YIELD											
AMOUNT											
PAY DATE											

DATE	TYPE		PRICE	QUANTITY #	COST	NET GAIN (LOSS)	AVERAGE COST	%
	BUY	SELL						
TOTAL GAIN (LOSS)					TOTAL% GAIN (LOSS)			%

TRADING NOTES

74

TICKER/SYMBOL

NAME

- ☐ STOCKS
- ☐ OPTIONS
- ☐ FUTURES
- ☐ OTHER:
- ☐ FOREX
- ☐ CRYPTO
- ☐ PENNY STOCKS

COMPANY PROFILE / NOTES

MARKET PLATFORMS	FEES

DIVIDEND (YES / NO)   ☐ QUARTERLY   ☐ YEARLY   ☐ MONTHLY

YIELD											
AMOUNT											
PAY DATE											

DATE	TYPE		PRICE	QUANTITY #	COST	NET GAIN (LOSS)	AVERAGE COST	%
	BUY	SELL						
TOTAL GAIN (LOSS)					TOTAL% GAIN (LOSS)			%

TRADING NOTES

TICKER/SYMBOL

NAME

- ☐ STOCKS
- ☐ OPTIONS
- ☐ FUTURES
- ☐ OTHER:
- ☐ FOREX
- ☐ CRYPTO
- ☐ PENNY STOCKS

COMPANY PROFILE / NOTES

MARKET PLATFORMS	FEES

DIVIDEND (YES / NO)   ☐ QUARTERLY   ☐ YEARLY   ☐ MONTHLY

YIELD											
AMOUNT											
PAY DATE											

DATE	TYPE		PRICE	QUANTITY #	COST	NET GAIN (LOSS)	AVERAGE COST	%
	BUY	SELL						
TOTAL GAIN (LOSS)					TOTAL% GAIN (LOSS)			%

TRADING NOTES

TICKER/SYMBOL

NAME

- ☐ STOCKS
- ☐ OPTIONS
- ☐ FUTURES
- ☐ OTHER:
- ☐ FOREX
- ☐ CRYPTO
- ☐ PENNY STOCKS

COMPANY PROFILE / NOTES

MARKET PLATFORMS	FEES

DIVIDEND (YES / NO)   ☐ QUARTERLY   ☐ YEARLY   ☐ MONTHLY

YIELD											
AMOUNT											
PAY DATE											

DATE	TYPE		PRICE	QUANTITY #	COST	NET GAIN (LOSS)	AVERAGE COST	%
	BUY	SELL						
TOTAL GAIN (LOSS)					TOTAL% GAIN (LOSS)			%

TRADING NOTES

TICKER/SYMBOL

NAME

- [ ] STOCKS
- [ ] OPTIONS
- [ ] FUTURES
- [ ] OTHER:
- [ ] FOREX
- [ ] CRYPTO
- [ ] PENNY STOCKS

COMPANY PROFILE / NOTES

MARKET PLATFORMS	FEES

DIVIDEND (YES / NO) [ ] QUARTERLY   [ ] YEARLY   [ ] MONTHLY

YIELD									
AMOUNT									
PAY DATE									

DATE	TYPE		PRICE	QUANTITY #	COST	NET GAIN (LOSS)	AVERAGE COST	%
	BUY	SELL						
TOTAL GAIN (LOSS)					TOTAL% GAIN (LOSS)			%

TRADING NOTES

TICKER/SYMBOL

NAME

- ☐ STOCKS
- ☐ OPTIONS
- ☐ FUTURES
- ☐ OTHER:
- ☐ FOREX
- ☐ CRYPTO
- ☐ PENNY STOCKS

COMPANY PROFILE / NOTES

MARKET PLATFORMS	FEES

DIVIDEND (YES / NO)   ☐ QUARTERLY   ☐ YEARLY   ☐ MONTHLY

YIELD										
AMOUNT										
PAY DATE										

DATE	TYPE		PRICE	QUANTITY #	COST	NET GAIN (LOSS)	AVERAGE COST	%
	BUY	SELL						
TOTAL GAIN (LOSS)					TOTAL% GAIN (LOSS)			%

TRADING NOTES

TICKER/SYMBOL

NAME

- [ ] STOCKS
- [ ] OPTIONS
- [ ] FUTURES
- [ ] OTHER:
- [ ] FOREX
- [ ] CRYPTO
- [ ] PENNY STOCKS

COMPANY PROFILE / NOTES

MARKET PLATFORMS	FEES

DIVIDEND (YES / NO)   [ ] QUARTERLY   [ ] YEARLY   [ ] MONTHLY

YIELD										
AMOUNT										
PAY DATE										

DATE	TYPE		PRICE	QUANTITY #	COST	NET GAIN (LOSS)	AVERAGE COST	%
	BUY	SELL						
TOTAL GAIN (LOSS)					TOTAL% GAIN (LOSS)			%

TRADING NOTES

TICKER/SYMBOL

NAME

- ☐ STOCKS
- ☐ OPTIONS
- ☐ FUTURES
- ☐ OTHER:
- ☐ FOREX
- ☐ CRYPTO
- ☐ PENNY STOCKS

COMPANY PROFILE / NOTES

MARKET PLATFORMS	FEES

DIVIDEND (YES / NO)   ☐ QUARTERLY   ☐ YEARLY   ☐ MONTHLY

YIELD										
AMOUNT										
PAY DATE										

DATE	TYPE		PRICE	QUANTITY #	COST	NET GAIN (LOSS)	AVERAGE COST	%
	BUY	SELL						
TOTAL GAIN (LOSS)					TOTAL% GAIN (LOSS)			%

TRADING NOTES

TICKER/SYMBOL

NAME

- ☐ STOCKS
- ☐ OPTIONS
- ☐ FUTURES
- ☐ OTHER:
- ☐ FOREX
- ☐ CRYPTO
- ☐ PENNY STOCKS

COMPANY PROFILE / NOTES

MARKET PLATFORMS	FEES

DIVIDEND (YES / NO)   ☐ QUARTERLY   ☐ YEARLY   ☐ MONTHLY

YIELD												
AMOUNT												
PAY DATE												

DATE	TYPE		PRICE	QUANTITY #	COST	NET GAIN (LOSS)	AVERAGE COST	%
	BUY	SELL						
TOTAL GAIN (LOSS)					TOTAL% GAIN (LOSS)			%

TRADING NOTES

TICKER/SYMBOL

NAME

- ☐ STOCKS
- ☐ OPTIONS
- ☐ FUTURES
- ☐ OTHER:
- ☐ FOREX
- ☐ CRYPTO
- ☐ PENNY STOCKS

COMPANY PROFILE / NOTES

MARKET PLATFORMS	FEES

DIVIDEND (YES / NO)   ☐ QUARTERLY   ☐ YEARLY   ☐ MONTHLY

YIELD										
AMOUNT										
PAY DATE										

DATE	TYPE		PRICE	QUANTITY #	COST	NET GAIN (LOSS)	AVERAGE COST	%
	BUY	SELL						
TOTAL GAIN (LOSS)					TOTAL% GAIN (LOSS)			%

TRADING NOTES

TICKER/SYMBOL

NAME

- ☐ STOCKS
- ☐ OPTIONS
- ☐ FUTURES
- ☐ OTHER:
- ☐ FOREX
- ☐ CRYPTO
- ☐ PENNY STOCKS

COMPANY PROFILE / NOTES

MARKET PLATFORMS	FEES

DIVIDEND (YES / NO)   ☐ QUARTERLY   ☐ YEARLY   ☐ MONTHLY

YIELD											
AMOUNT											
PAY DATE											

DATE	TYPE		PRICE	QUANTITY #	COST	NET GAIN (LOSS)	AVERAGE COST	%
	BUY	SELL						
TOTAL GAIN (LOSS)					TOTAL% GAIN (LOSS)			%

TRADING NOTES

TICKER/SYMBOL	NAME

- [ ] STOCKS
- [ ] OPTIONS
- [ ] FUTURES
- [ ] OTHER:
- [ ] FOREX
- [ ] CRYPTO
- [ ] PENNY STOCKS

COMPANY PROFILE / NOTES

MARKET PLATFORMS	FEES

DIVIDEND (YES / NO)   ☐ QUARTERLY   ☐ YEARLY   ☐ MONTHLY

YIELD											
AMOUNT											
PAY DATE											

DATE	TYPE		PRICE	QUANTITY #	COST	NET GAIN (LOSS)	AVERAGE COST	%
	BUY	SELL						
TOTAL GAIN (LOSS)					**TOTAL% GAIN (LOSS)**			%

TRADING NOTES

STOCKS WATCHLIST

TICKER/SYMBOL

NAME

- [ ] STOCKS
- [ ] OPTIONS
- [ ] FUTURES
- [ ] OTHER:
- [ ] FOREX
- [ ] CRYPTO
- [ ] PENNY STOCKS

COMPANY PROFILE / SECTOR

MARKET CAP	P/E	VOLUME	52 Wk Low	52 Wk High	MARKET (PRICE)	LIMIT/WISH (PRICE)

DIVIDEND (YES / NO) [ ] QUARTERLY [ ] YEARLY [ ] MONTHLY YIELD ____ AMOUNT ____

NOTES

TICKER/SYMBOL

NAME

- [ ] STOCKS
- [ ] OPTIONS
- [ ] FUTURES
- [ ] OTHER:
- [ ] FOREX
- [ ] CRYPTO
- [ ] PENNY STOCKS

COMPANY PROFILE / SECTOR

MARKET CAP	P/E	VOLUME	52 Wk Low	52 Wk High	MARKET (PRICE)	LIMIT/WISH (PRICE)

DIVIDEND (YES / NO) [ ] QUARTERLY [ ] YEARLY [ ] MONTHLY YIELD ____ AMOUNT ____

NOTES

STOCKS WATCHLIST

TICKER/SYMBOL

NAME

- [ ] STOCKS
- [ ] OPTIONS
- [ ] FUTURES
- [ ] OTHER:
- [ ] FOREX
- [ ] CRYPTO
- [ ] PENNY STOCKS

COMPANY PROFILE / SECTOR

MARKET CAP	P/E	VOLUME	52 Wk Low	52 Wk High	MARKET (PRICE)	LIMIT/WISH (PRICE)

DIVIDEND (YES / NO) ☐ QUARTERLY ☐ YEARLY ☐ MONTHLY   YIELD _____   AMOUNT _____

NOTES

TICKER/SYMBOL

NAME

- [ ] STOCKS
- [ ] OPTIONS
- [ ] FUTURES
- [ ] OTHER:
- [ ] FOREX
- [ ] CRYPTO
- [ ] PENNY STOCKS

COMPANY PROFILE / SECTOR

MARKET CAP	P/E	VOLUME	52 Wk Low	52 Wk High	MARKET (PRICE)	LIMIT/WISH (PRICE)

DIVIDEND (YES / NO) ☐ QUARTERLY ☐ YEARLY ☐ MONTHLY   YIELD _____   AMOUNT _____

NOTES

STOCKS WATCHLIST

TICKER/SYMBOL | NAME

☐ STOCKS ☐ FOREX
☐ OPTIONS ☐ CRYPTO
☐ FUTURES ☐ PENNY STOCKS
☐ OTHER:

COMPANY PROFILE / SECTOR

MARKET CAP	P/E	VOLUME	52 Wk Low	52 Wk High	MARKET (PRICE)	LIMIT/WISH (PRICE)

DIVIDEND (YES / NO) ☐ QUARTERLY ☐ YEARLY ☐ MONTHLY   YIELD AMOUNT

NOTES

TICKER/SYMBOL | NAME

☐ STOCKS ☐ FOREX
☐ OPTIONS ☐ CRYPTO
☐ FUTURES ☐ PENNY STOCKS
☐ OTHER:

COMPANY PROFILE / SECTOR

MARKET CAP	P/E	VOLUME	52 Wk Low	52 Wk High	MARKET (PRICE)	LIMIT/WISH (PRICE)

DIVIDEND (YES / NO) ☐ QUARTERLY ☐ YEARLY ☐ MONTHLY   YIELD AMOUNT

NOTES

STOCKS WATCHLIST

TICKER/SYMBOL

NAME

- ☐ STOCKS
- ☐ OPTIONS
- ☐ FUTURES
- ☐ OTHER:
- ☐ FOREX
- ☐ CRYPTO
- ☐ PENNY STOCKS

COMPANY PROFILE / SECTOR

MARKET CAP	P/E	VOLUME	52 Wk Low	52 Wk High	MARKET (PRICE)	LIMIT/WISH (PRICE)

DIVIDEND (YES / NO) ☐ QUARTERLY ☐ YEARLY ☐ MONTHLY   YIELD ☐   AMOUNT ☐

NOTES

TICKER/SYMBOL

NAME

- ☐ STOCKS
- ☐ OPTIONS
- ☐ FUTURES
- ☐ OTHER:
- ☐ FOREX
- ☐ CRYPTO
- ☐ PENNY STOCKS

COMPANY PROFILE / SECTOR

MARKET CAP	P/E	VOLUME	52 Wk Low	52 Wk High	MARKET (PRICE)	LIMIT/WISH (PRICE)

DIVIDEND (YES / NO) ☐ QUARTERLY ☐ YEARLY ☐ MONTHLY   YIELD ☐   AMOUNT ☐

NOTES

STOCKS WATCHLIST

TICKER/SYMBOL

NAME

- ☐ STOCKS
- ☐ OPTIONS
- ☐ FUTURES
- ☐ OTHER:
- ☐ FOREX
- ☐ CRYPTO
- ☐ PENNY STOCKS

COMPANY PROFILE / SECTOR

MARKET CAP	P/E	VOLUME	52 Wk Low	52 Wk High	MARKET (PRICE)	LIMIT/WISH (PRICE)

DIVIDEND (YES / NO) ☐ QUARTERLY ☐ YEARLY ☐ MONTHLY   YIELD ☐ AMOUNT

NOTES

TICKER/SYMBOL

NAME

- ☐ STOCKS
- ☐ OPTIONS
- ☐ FUTURES
- ☐ OTHER:
- ☐ FOREX
- ☐ CRYPTO
- ☐ PENNY STOCKS

COMPANY PROFILE / SECTOR

MARKET CAP	P/E	VOLUME	52 Wk Low	52 Wk High	MARKET (PRICE)	LIMIT/WISH (PRICE)

DIVIDEND (YES / NO) ☐ QUARTERLY ☐ YEARLY ☐ MONTHLY   YIELD ☐ AMOUNT

NOTES

STOCKS WATCHLIST

TICKER/SYMBOL

NAME

- [ ] STOCKS
- [ ] OPTIONS
- [ ] FUTURES
- [ ] OTHER:
- [ ] FOREX
- [ ] CRYPTO
- [ ] PENNY STOCKS

COMPANY PROFILE / SECTOR

MARKET CAP	P/E	VOLUME	52 Wk Low	52 Wk High	MARKET (PRICE)	LIMIT/WISH (PRICE)

DIVIDEND (YES / NO) [ ] QUARTERLY [ ] YEARLY [ ] MONTHLY YIELD   AMOUNT

NOTES

TICKER/SYMBOL

NAME

- [ ] STOCKS
- [ ] OPTIONS
- [ ] FUTURES
- [ ] OTHER:
- [ ] FOREX
- [ ] CRYPTO
- [ ] PENNY STOCKS

COMPANY PROFILE / SECTOR

MARKET CAP	P/E	VOLUME	52 Wk Low	52 Wk High	MARKET (PRICE)	LIMIT/WISH (PRICE)

DIVIDEND (YES / NO) [ ] QUARTERLY [ ] YEARLY [ ] MONTHLY YIELD   AMOUNT

NOTES

STOCKS WATCHLIST

TICKER/SYMBOL

NAME

- [ ] STOCKS
- [ ] OPTIONS
- [ ] FUTURES
- [ ] OTHER:
- [ ] FOREX
- [ ] CRYPTO
- [ ] PENNY STOCKS

COMPANY PROFILE / SECTOR

MARKET CAP	P/E	VOLUME	52 Wk Low	52 Wk High	MARKET (PRICE)	LIMIT/WISH (PRICE)

DIVIDEND (YES / NO) [ ] QUARTERLY [ ] YEARLY [ ] MONTHLY YIELD ____ AMOUNT ____

NOTES

TICKER/SYMBOL

NAME

- [ ] STOCKS
- [ ] OPTIONS
- [ ] FUTURES
- [ ] OTHER:
- [ ] FOREX
- [ ] CRYPTO
- [ ] PENNY STOCKS

COMPANY PROFILE / SECTOR

MARKET CAP	P/E	VOLUME	52 Wk Low	52 Wk High	MARKET (PRICE)	LIMIT/WISH (PRICE)

DIVIDEND (YES / NO) [ ] QUARTERLY [ ] YEARLY [ ] MONTHLY YIELD ____ AMOUNT ____

NOTES

STOCKS WATCHLIST

TICKER/SYMBOL

NAME

- [ ] STOCKS
- [ ] OPTIONS
- [ ] FUTURES
- [ ] OTHER:
- [ ] FOREX
- [ ] CRYPTO
- [ ] PENNY STOCKS

COMPANY PROFILE / SECTOR

MARKET CAP	P/E	VOLUME	52 Wk Low	52 Wk High	MARKET (PRICE)	LIMIT/WISH (PRICE)

DIVIDEND (YES / NO) [ ] QUARTERLY [ ] YEARLY [ ] MONTHLY   YIELD _____   AMOUNT _____

NOTES

TICKER/SYMBOL

NAME

- [ ] STOCKS
- [ ] OPTIONS
- [ ] FUTURES
- [ ] OTHER:
- [ ] FOREX
- [ ] CRYPTO
- [ ] PENNY STOCKS

COMPANY PROFILE / SECTOR

MARKET CAP	P/E	VOLUME	52 Wk Low	52 Wk High	MARKET (PRICE)	LIMIT/WISH (PRICE)

DIVIDEND (YES / NO) [ ] QUARTERLY [ ] YEARLY [ ] MONTHLY   YIELD _____   AMOUNT _____

NOTES

STOCKS WATCHLIST

TICKER/SYMBOL | NAME

- ☐ STOCKS
- ☐ OPTIONS
- ☐ FUTURES
- ☐ OTHER:
- ☐ FOREX
- ☐ CRYPTO
- ☐ PENNY STOCKS

COMPANY PROFILE / SECTOR

MARKET CAP	P/E	VOLUME	52 Wk Low	52 Wk High	MARKET (PRICE)	LIMIT/WISH (PRICE)

DIVIDEND (YES / NO) ☐ QUARTERLY ☐ YEARLY ☐ MONTHLY YIELD _____ AMOUNT _____

NOTES

TICKER/SYMBOL | NAME

- ☐ STOCKS
- ☐ OPTIONS
- ☐ FUTURES
- ☐ OTHER:
- ☐ FOREX
- ☐ CRYPTO
- ☐ PENNY STOCKS

COMPANY PROFILE / SECTOR

MARKET CAP	P/E	VOLUME	52 Wk Low	52 Wk High	MARKET (PRICE)	LIMIT/WISH (PRICE)

DIVIDEND (YES / NO) ☐ QUARTERLY ☐ YEARLY ☐ MONTHLY YIELD _____ AMOUNT _____

NOTES

STOCKS WATCHLIST

TICKER/SYMBOL

NAME

- ☐ STOCKS
- ☐ OPTIONS
- ☐ FUTURES
- ☐ OTHER:
- ☐ FOREX
- ☐ CRYPTO
- ☐ PENNY STOCKS

COMPANY PROFILE / SECTOR

MARKET CAP	P/E	VOLUME	52 Wk Low	52 Wk High	MARKET (PRICE)	LIMIT/WISH (PRICE)

DIVIDEND (YES / NO) ☐ QUARTERLY ☐ YEARLY ☐ MONTHLY   YIELD _____ AMOUNT _____

NOTES

TICKER/SYMBOL

NAME

- ☐ STOCKS
- ☐ OPTIONS
- ☐ FUTURES
- ☐ OTHER:
- ☐ FOREX
- ☐ CRYPTO
- ☐ PENNY STOCKS

COMPANY PROFILE / SECTOR

MARKET CAP	P/E	VOLUME	52 Wk Low	52 Wk High	MARKET (PRICE)	LIMIT/WISH (PRICE)

DIVIDEND (YES / NO) ☐ QUARTERLY ☐ YEARLY ☐ MONTHLY   YIELD _____ AMOUNT _____

NOTES

STOCKS WATCHLIST

TICKER/SYMBOL | NAME

- [ ] STOCKS
- [ ] OPTIONS
- [ ] FUTURES
- [ ] OTHER:
- [ ] FOREX
- [ ] CRYPTO
- [ ] PENNY STOCKS

COMPANY PROFILE / SECTOR

MARKET CAP	P/E	VOLUME	52 Wk Low	52 Wk High	MARKET (PRICE)	LIMIT/WISH (PRICE)

DIVIDEND (YES / NO) [ ] QUARTERLY [ ] YEARLY [ ] MONTHLY YIELD _____ AMOUNT _____

NOTES

TICKER/SYMBOL | NAME

- [ ] STOCKS
- [ ] OPTIONS
- [ ] FUTURES
- [ ] OTHER:
- [ ] FOREX
- [ ] CRYPTO
- [ ] PENNY STOCKS

COMPANY PROFILE / SECTOR

MARKET CAP	P/E	VOLUME	52 Wk Low	52 Wk High	MARKET (PRICE)	LIMIT/WISH (PRICE)

DIVIDEND (YES / NO) [ ] QUARTERLY [ ] YEARLY [ ] MONTHLY YIELD _____ AMOUNT _____

NOTES

STOCKS WATCHLIST

TICKER/SYMBOL   NAME

- [ ] STOCKS   [ ] FOREX
- [ ] OPTIONS   [ ] CRYPTO
- [ ] FUTURES   [ ] PENNY STOCKS
- [ ] OTHER:

COMPANY PROFILE / SECTOR

MARKET CAP	P/E	VOLUME	52 Wk Low	52 Wk High	MARKET (PRICE)	LIMIT/WISH (PRICE)

DIVIDEND (YES / NO) [ ] QUARTERLY [ ] YEARLY [ ] MONTHLY   YIELD   AMOUNT

NOTES

TICKER/SYMBOL   NAME

- [ ] STOCKS   [ ] FOREX
- [ ] OPTIONS   [ ] CRYPTO
- [ ] FUTURES   [ ] PENNY STOCKS
- [ ] OTHER:

COMPANY PROFILE / SECTOR

MARKET CAP	P/E	VOLUME	52 Wk Low	52 Wk High	MARKET (PRICE)	LIMIT/WISH (PRICE)

DIVIDEND (YES / NO) [ ] QUARTERLY [ ] YEARLY [ ] MONTHLY   YIELD   AMOUNT

NOTES

STOCKS WATCHLIST

TICKER/SYMBOL | NAME

- ☐ STOCKS   ☐ FOREX
- ☐ OPTIONS   ☐ CRYPTO
- ☐ FUTURES   ☐ PENNY STOCKS
- ☐ OTHER:

COMPANY PROFILE / SECTOR

MARKET CAP	P/E	VOLUME	52 Wk Low	52 Wk High	MARKET (PRICE)	LIMIT/WISH (PRICE)

DIVIDEND (YES / NO) ☐ QUARTERLY ☐ YEARLY ☐ MONTHLY   YIELD ☐   AMOUNT ☐

NOTES

TICKER/SYMBOL | NAME

- ☐ STOCKS   ☐ FOREX
- ☐ OPTIONS   ☐ CRYPTO
- ☐ FUTURES   ☐ PENNY STOCKS
- ☐ OTHER:

COMPANY PROFILE / SECTOR

MARKET CAP	P/E	VOLUME	52 Wk Low	52 Wk High	MARKET (PRICE)	LIMIT/WISH (PRICE)

DIVIDEND (YES / NO) ☐ QUARTERLY ☐ YEARLY ☐ MONTHLY   YIELD ☐   AMOUNT ☐

NOTES

STOCKS WATCHLIST

TICKER/SYMBOL	NAME

		COMPANY PROFILE / SECTOR
☐ STOCKS ☐ FOREX		
☐ OPTIONS ☐ CRYPTO		
☐ FUTURES ☐ PENNY STOCKS		
☐ OTHER:		

MARKET CAP	P/E	VOLUME	52 Wk Low	52 Wk High	MARKET (PRICE)	LIMIT/WISH (PRICE)

DIVIDEND (YES / NO) ☐ QUARTERLY ☐ YEARLY ☐ MONTHLY   YIELD _____   AMOUNT _____

NOTES

TICKER/SYMBOL	NAME

		COMPANY PROFILE / SECTOR
☐ STOCKS ☐ FOREX		
☐ OPTIONS ☐ CRYPTO		
☐ FUTURES ☐ PENNY STOCKS		
☐ OTHER:		

MARKET CAP	P/E	VOLUME	52 Wk Low	52 Wk High	MARKET (PRICE)	LIMIT/WISH (PRICE)

DIVIDEND (YES / NO) ☐ QUARTERLY ☐ YEARLY ☐ MONTHLY   YIELD _____   AMOUNT _____

NOTES

STOCKS WATCHLIST

TICKER/SYMBOL | NAME

- ☐ STOCKS
- ☐ OPTIONS
- ☐ FUTURES
- ☐ OTHER:
- ☐ FOREX
- ☐ CRYPTO
- ☐ PENNY STOCKS

COMPANY PROFILE / SECTOR

MARKET CAP	P/E	VOLUME	52 Wk Low	52 Wk High	MARKET (PRICE)	LIMIT/WISH (PRICE)

DIVIDEND (YES / NO) ☐ QUARTERLY ☐ YEARLY ☐ MONTHLY YIELD ____ AMOUNT ____

NOTES

TICKER/SYMBOL | NAME

- ☐ STOCKS
- ☐ OPTIONS
- ☐ FUTURES
- ☐ OTHER:
- ☐ FOREX
- ☐ CRYPTO
- ☐ PENNY STOCKS

COMPANY PROFILE / SECTOR

MARKET CAP	P/E	VOLUME	52 Wk Low	52 Wk High	MARKET (PRICE)	LIMIT/WISH (PRICE)

DIVIDEND (YES / NO) ☐ QUARTERLY ☐ YEARLY ☐ MONTHLY YIELD ____ AMOUNT ____

NOTES

STOCKS WATCHLIST

TICKER/SYMBOL	NAME

	COMPANY PROFILE / SECTOR
☐ STOCKS ☐ FOREX	
☐ OPTIONS ☐ CRYPTO	
☐ FUTURES ☐ PENNY STOCKS	
☐ OTHER:	

MARKET CAP	P/E	VOLUME	52 Wk Low	52 Wk High	MARKET (PRICE)	LIMIT/WISH (PRICE)

DIVIDEND (YES / NO) ☐ QUARTERLY ☐ YEARLY ☐ MONTHLY   YIELD [ ]   AMOUNT [ ]

NOTES

TICKER/SYMBOL	NAME

	COMPANY PROFILE / SECTOR
☐ STOCKS ☐ FOREX	
☐ OPTIONS ☐ CRYPTO	
☐ FUTURES ☐ PENNY STOCKS	
☐ OTHER:	

MARKET CAP	P/E	VOLUME	52 Wk Low	52 Wk High	MARKET (PRICE)	LIMIT/WISH (PRICE)

DIVIDEND (YES / NO) ☐ QUARTERLY ☐ YEARLY ☐ MONTHLY   YIELD [ ]   AMOUNT [ ]

NOTES

STOCKS WATCHLIST

TICKER/SYMBOL	NAME

		COMPANY PROFILE / SECTOR
☐ STOCKS	☐ FOREX	
☐ OPTIONS	☐ CRYPTO	
☐ FUTURES	☐ PENNY STOCKS	
☐ OTHER:		

MARKET CAP	P/E	VOLUME	52 Wk Low	52 Wk High	MARKET (PRICE)	LIMIT/WISH (PRICE)

DIVIDEND (YES / NO) ☐ QUARTERLY ☐ YEARLY ☐ MONTHLY   YIELD [ ]   AMOUNT [ ]

NOTES

TICKER/SYMBOL	NAME

		COMPANY PROFILE / SECTOR
☐ STOCKS	☐ FOREX	
☐ OPTIONS	☐ CRYPTO	
☐ FUTURES	☐ PENNY STOCKS	
☐ OTHER:		

MARKET CAP	P/E	VOLUME	52 Wk Low	52 Wk High	MARKET (PRICE)	LIMIT/WISH (PRICE)

DIVIDEND (YES / NO) ☐ QUARTERLY ☐ YEARLY ☐ MONTHLY   YIELD [ ]   AMOUNT [ ]

NOTES

STOCKS WATCHLIST

TICKER/SYMBOL

NAME

- ☐ STOCKS
- ☐ OPTIONS
- ☐ FUTURES
- ☐ OTHER:
- ☐ FOREX
- ☐ CRYPTO
- ☐ PENNY STOCKS

COMPANY PROFILE / SECTOR

MARKET CAP	P/E	VOLUME	52 Wk Low	52 Wk High	MARKET (PRICE)	LIMIT/WISH (PRICE)

DIVIDEND (YES / NO) ☐ QUARTERLY ☐ YEARLY ☐ MONTHLY YIELD [ ] AMOUNT [ ]

NOTES

TICKER/SYMBOL

NAME

- ☐ STOCKS
- ☐ OPTIONS
- ☐ FUTURES
- ☐ OTHER:
- ☐ FOREX
- ☐ CRYPTO
- ☐ PENNY STOCKS

COMPANY PROFILE / SECTOR

MARKET CAP	P/E	VOLUME	52 Wk Low	52 Wk High	MARKET (PRICE)	LIMIT/WISH (PRICE)

DIVIDEND (YES / NO) ☐ QUARTERLY ☐ YEARLY ☐ MONTHLY YIELD [ ] AMOUNT [ ]

NOTES

STOCKS WATCHLIST

TICKER/SYMBOL

NAME

- ☐ STOCKS
- ☐ OPTIONS
- ☐ FUTURES
- ☐ OTHER:
- ☐ FOREX
- ☐ CRYPTO
- ☐ PENNY STOCKS

COMPANY PROFILE / SECTOR

MARKET CAP	P/E	VOLUME	52 Wk Low	52 Wk High	MARKET (PRICE)	LIMIT/WISH (PRICE)

DIVIDEND (YES / NO) ☐ QUARTERLY ☐ YEARLY ☐ MONTHLY   YIELD _____   AMOUNT _____

NOTES

TICKER/SYMBOL

NAME

- ☐ STOCKS
- ☐ OPTIONS
- ☐ FUTURES
- ☐ OTHER:
- ☐ FOREX
- ☐ CRYPTO
- ☐ PENNY STOCKS

COMPANY PROFILE / SECTOR

MARKET CAP	P/E	VOLUME	52 Wk Low	52 Wk High	MARKET (PRICE)	LIMIT/WISH (PRICE)

DIVIDEND (YES / NO) ☐ QUARTERLY ☐ YEARLY ☐ MONTHLY   YIELD _____   AMOUNT _____

NOTES

STOCKS WATCHLIST

TICKER/SYMBOL

NAME

- [ ] STOCKS
- [ ] OPTIONS
- [ ] FUTURES
- [ ] OTHER:
- [ ] FOREX
- [ ] CRYPTO
- [ ] PENNY STOCKS

COMPANY PROFILE / SECTOR

MARKET CAP	P/E	VOLUME	52 Wk Low	52 Wk High	MARKET (PRICE)	LIMIT/WISH (PRICE)

DIVIDEND (YES / NO) [ ] QUARTERLY [ ] YEARLY [ ] MONTHLY   YIELD   AMOUNT

NOTES

TICKER/SYMBOL

NAME

- [ ] STOCKS
- [ ] OPTIONS
- [ ] FUTURES
- [ ] OTHER:
- [ ] FOREX
- [ ] CRYPTO
- [ ] PENNY STOCKS

COMPANY PROFILE / SECTOR

MARKET CAP	P/E	VOLUME	52 Wk Low	52 Wk High	MARKET (PRICE)	LIMIT/WISH (PRICE)

DIVIDEND (YES / NO) [ ] QUARTERLY [ ] YEARLY [ ] MONTHLY   YIELD   AMOUNT

NOTES

TRADING NOTES

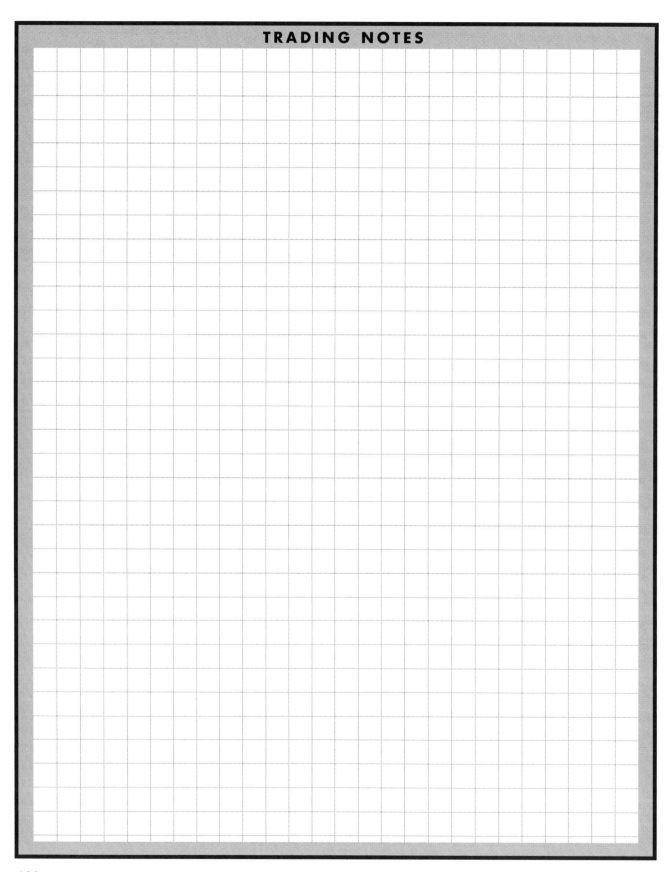

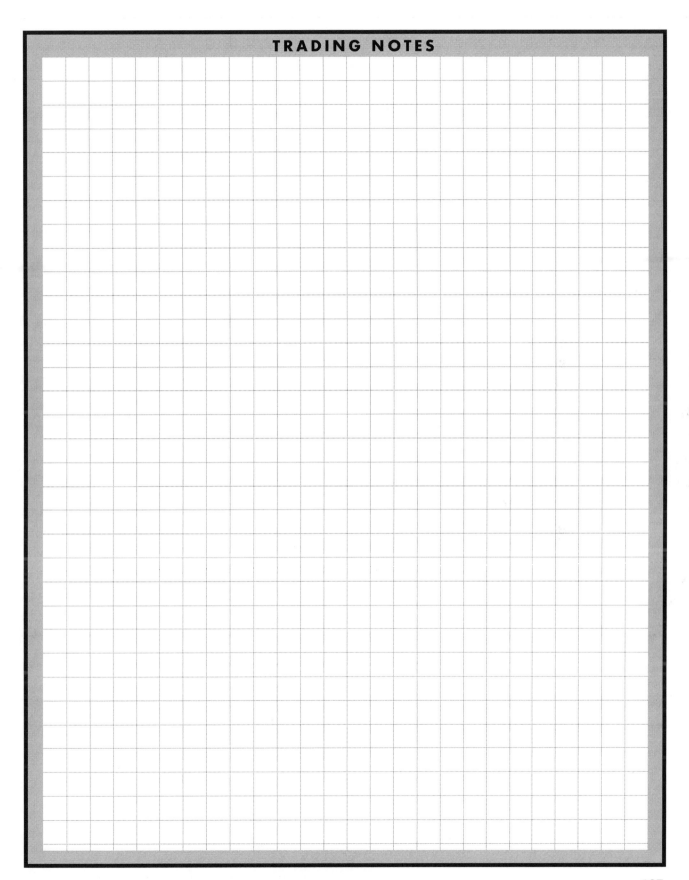

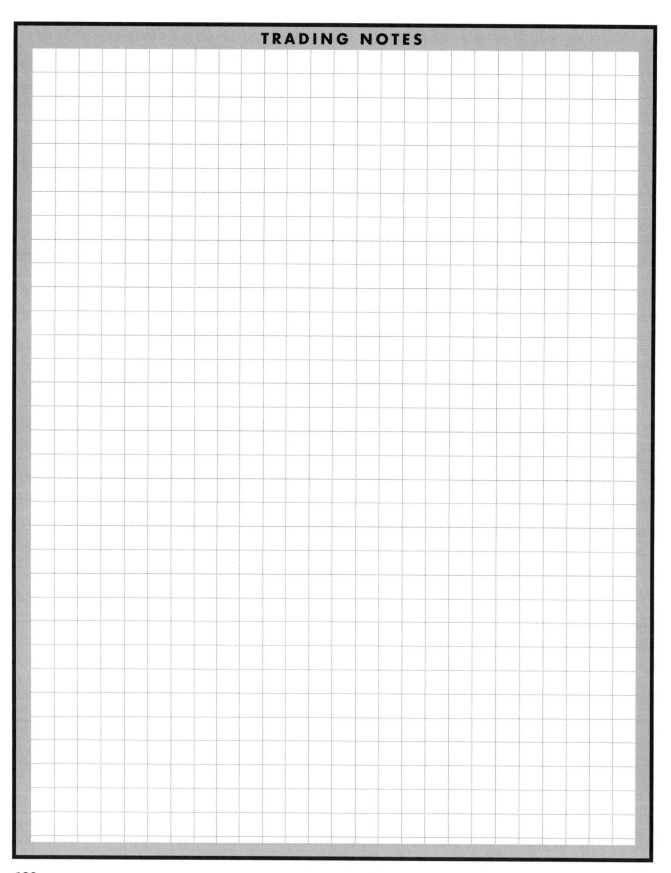

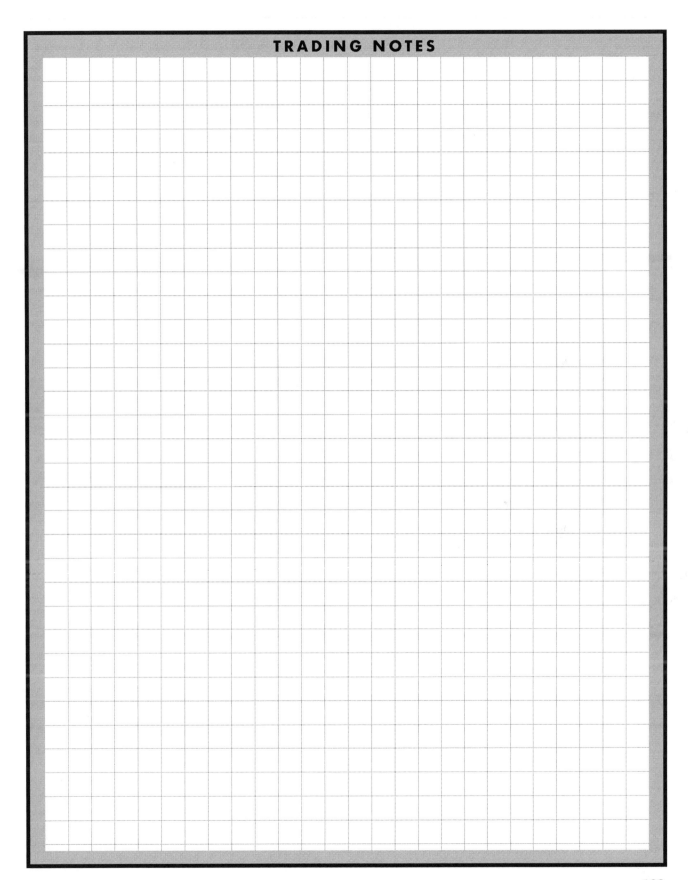

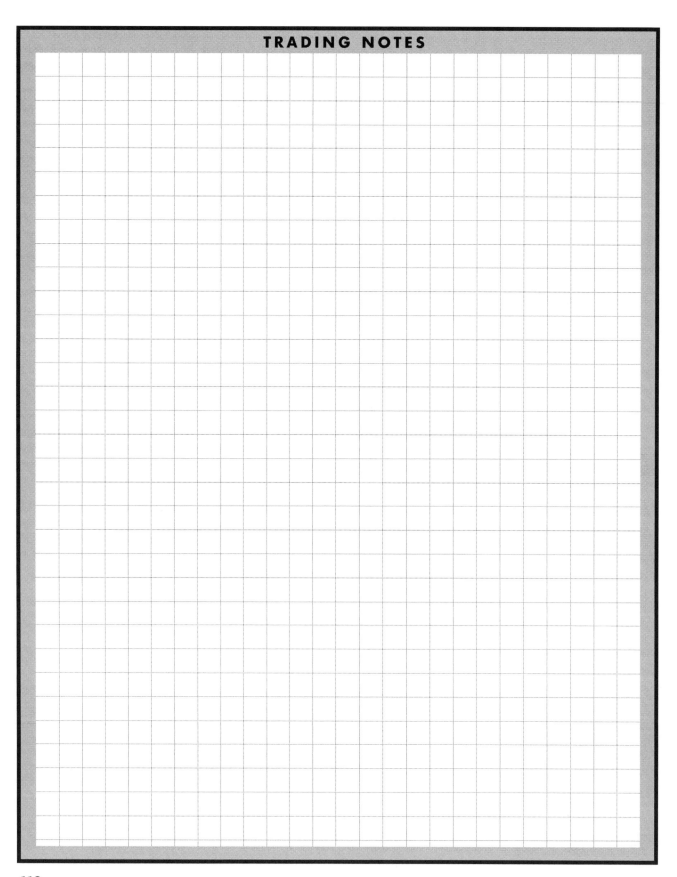

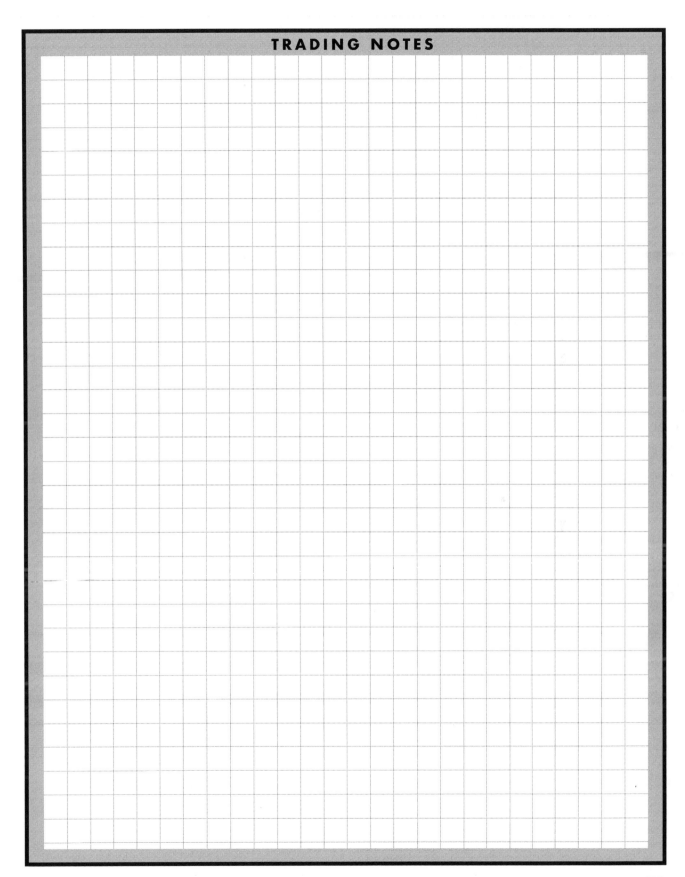

TRADING NOTES

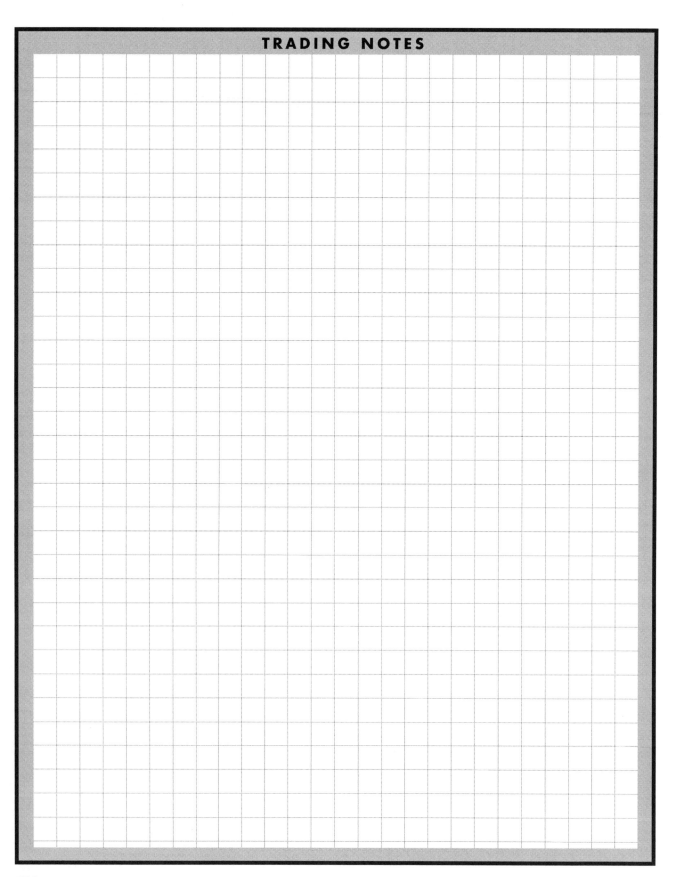

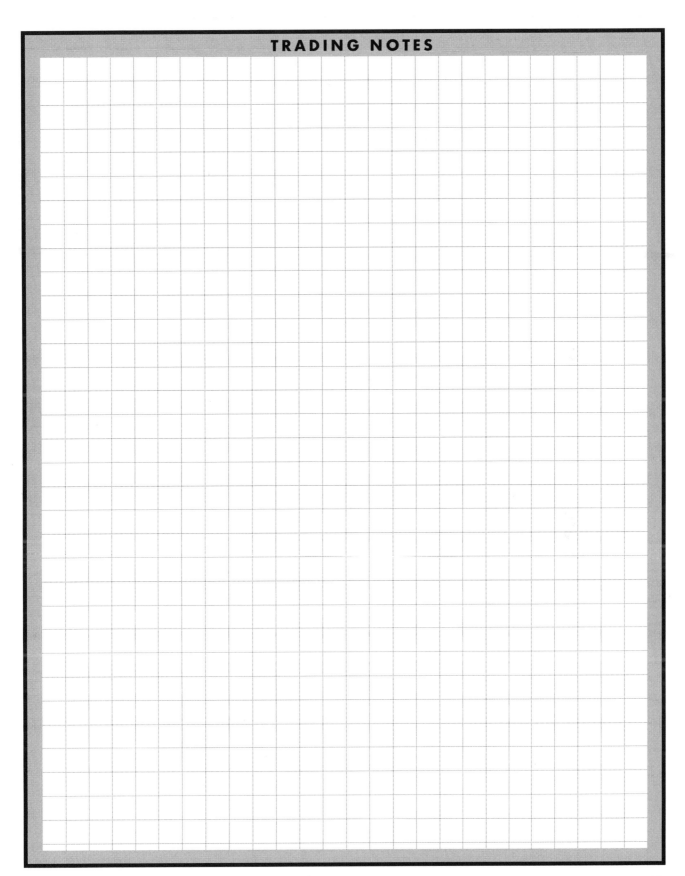

TRADING NOTES

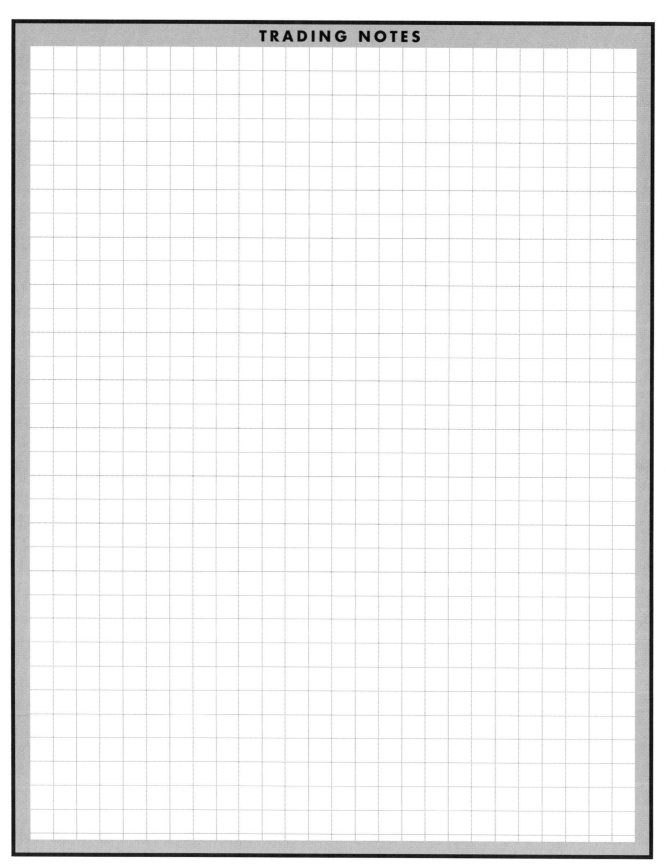

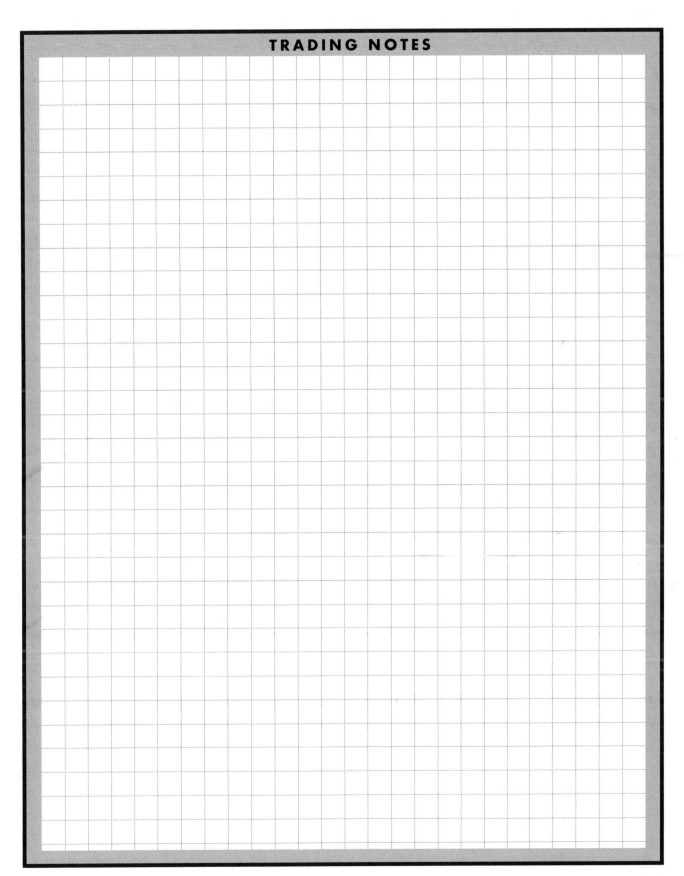

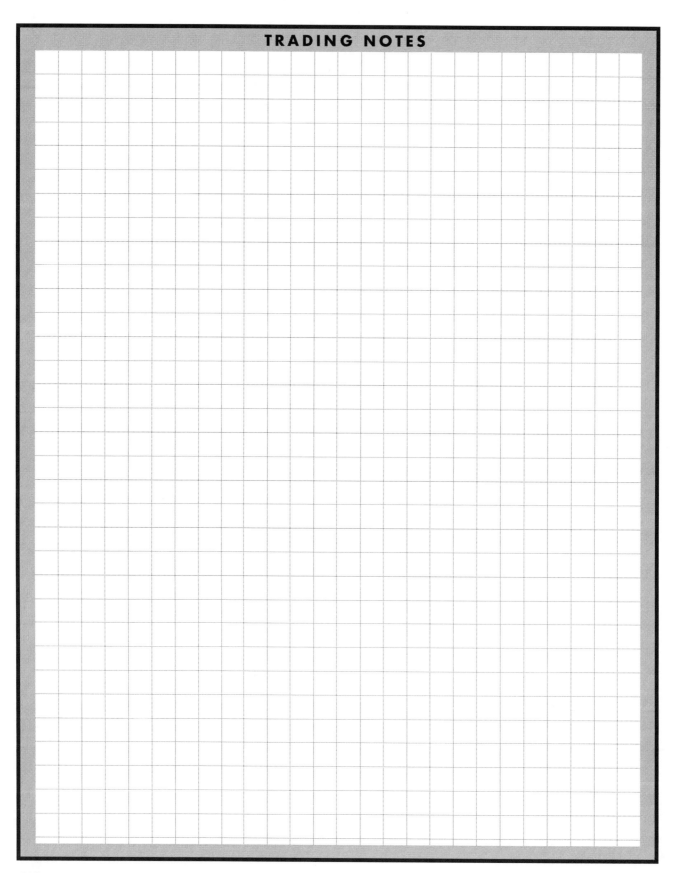

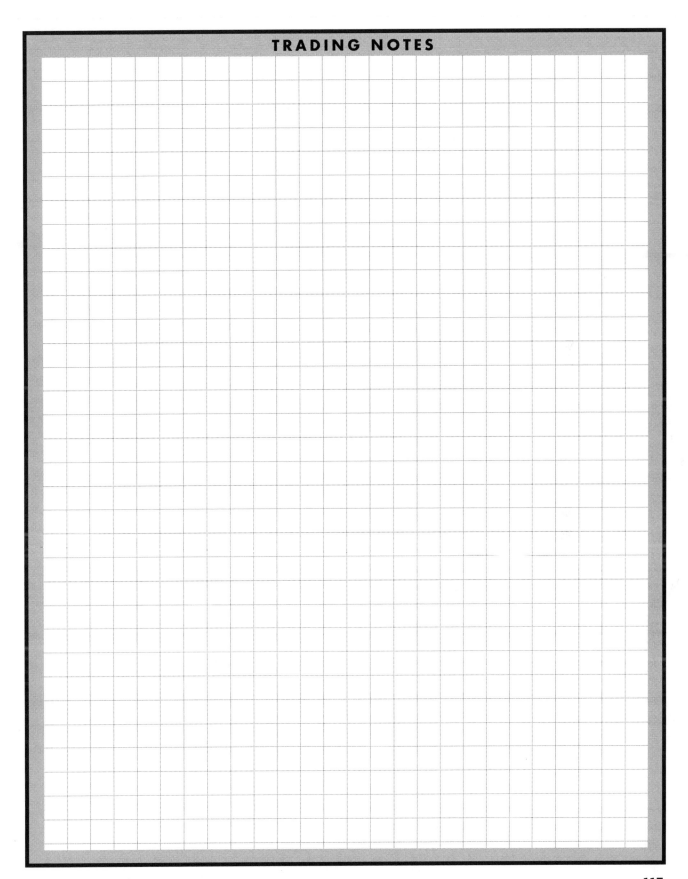

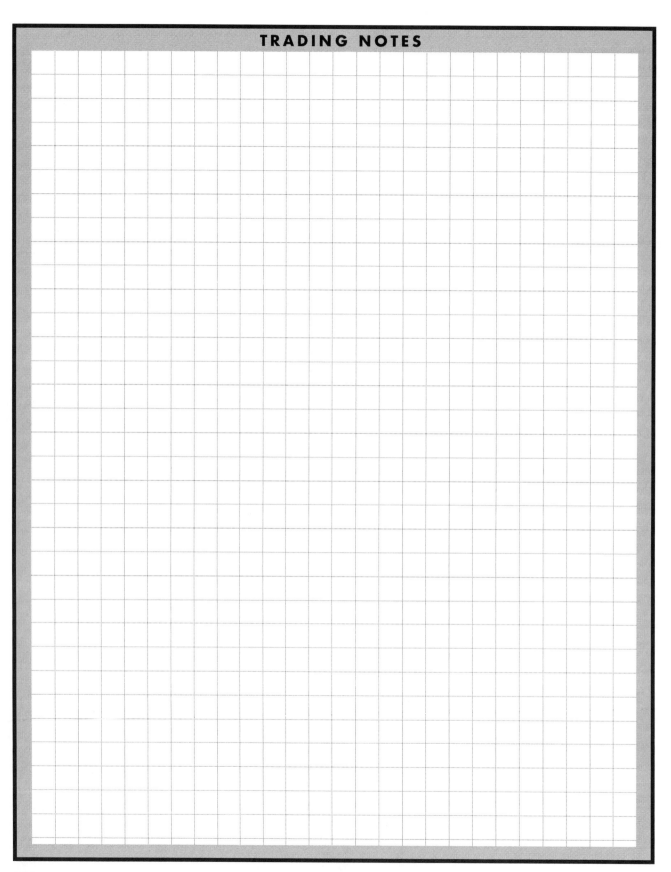

MONTHLY
TRADING PROFIT RESULTS

MONTH	GOAL	RESULT

Thank you for choosing 'Trading Journal'.
Your comments and reviews will encourage us to make better stock notebooks.
I hope you always buy the dips and sell the rips!

Made in United States
Orlando, FL
05 December 2024

55017694R00074